BIRDWATCHING WALKS IN CUMBRIA

Birdwatching Walks in Cumbria

Tim Dean
and
Jeremy Roberts

Carnegie Publishing Ltd

© Tim Dean and Jeremy Roberts, 2002

Published by Carnegie Publishing Ltd,
Carnegie House,
Chatsworth Road,
Lancaster LA1 4SL
Tel: 01524 840111
Fax: 01524 840222
email: carnegie@provider.co.uk
publishing and book sales: www.carnegiepub.co.uk
book production: www.wooof.net

First edition, 2002

British Library Cataloguing-in-Publication data
A catalogue record for this book is available from the British Library

ISBN 1 85936 074 2

Typeset by Carnegie Publishing
Printed by Cromwell Press, Wiltshire

Dedicated to all birdwatching walkers

Contents

Preface

What better place in England to combine walking and birdwatching than Cumbria!

Walking in the county is a well-known pleasure. Cumbrian scenery is breathtaking; poetry, prose and art and the legions of walkers are testament to this. Birdwatching in the county is a pleasure less widely known – but one which should be shared and savoured.

Cumbria is a big county and it is doubtful whether any other in England has a greater variety of habitats: from England's highest mountains via becks, wooded valleys and broad rivers to the wide expanses of the Solway Firth, Duddon Estuary and Morecambe Bay and from England's largest lake via moorland, farmland and industry to the impressive sandstone cliffs at St Bees Head. A network of tracks, paths and bridleways leads you to places where waders and wildfowl can be seen in their thousands, where Buzzards 'sky-dance', and where Puffins, Razorbills, Guillemots and Kittiwakes jostle for space.

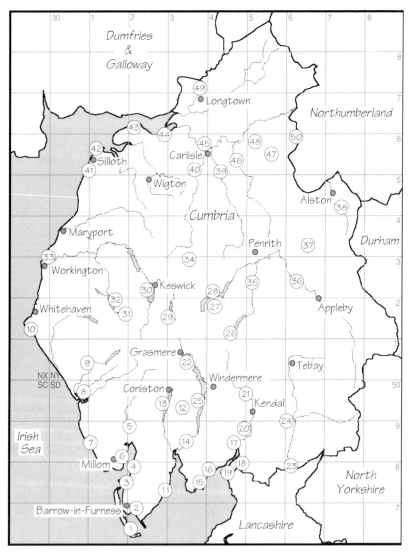

Location Map for Bird Walks

The numbers refer to the walks in the book e.g. 11 Bardsea and Baycliff

Introduction

These fifty walks are easy-paced and finish where they start. Each walk is illustrated by a rough sketch-map to be used in conjunction with the text. The distances are approximate and all the walks are on official rights-of-way, permissive footpaths or public access areas. Paths can, however, be legally changed from time to time, in which case there should be a sign specifically indicating any alteration.

A study of tide tables is essential to make the most out of some coastal walks, and for your own safety.

Maps

We strongly advise you to carry the relevant OS map, mentioned with each walk. The *Landranger* series, at 1:50,000, will often provide you with sufficient detail. However, the 1:25,000 mapping used in the superb *Outdoor Leisure* maps, which cover many of the walks, and the *Pathfinder* series which cover the rest, really will enhance your enjoyment still more, by providing much extra information not given on our sketch-maps, and by detailing other possible routes you might want (or in some circumstances, need) to take.

Route-finding and safety considerations

In most cases, the path you follow will be obvious on the ground. Often there will be footpath signs or way-markers. There are exceptions, however, such as some paths over open moorland or mountain. You must not attempt our high-level walks unless you are experienced in mountain walking. Cumbria's fickle weather in all seasons must not be under-estimated. You need good walking gear, from worn-in boots up to headware, provisions, contingency equipment, direction-finding equipment and a knowledge of how to use it. The GPS (Global Positioning System) receiver is now becoming affordable, and – with compass and map – can be a real help in route-finding, especially if the mist comes down.

(You will have read about the problems caused to the rescue services by hill-walking parties having relied upon the ubiquitous mobile phone, rather than the right experience, knowledge and equipment. Don't fall into that trap: you'll often be out of reception in the hills, in any case!)

What to wear

Clothing of course is a matter of choice, but always carry weather-proof gear even when the day seems fair. For watching birds close-up, discreet and 'noiseless' clothing is infinitely preferable to a fluorescent and rustling cagoule that can be seen and heard from the Isle of Man.

Cumbria being generally wet, many of our walks are along paths which may be muddy. Wellingtons (for lowland walks) or boots are usually the best footware. Clean trainers will not remain so!

Optical equipment and its use

Always have your binoculars out and ready to use. Many beginners, or casual bird-watchers, carry around their binoculars in the original case, or worse, in the case in the rucksack (or worse yet, leave both of them in the car!), intending to get them out 'when they find a bird to look at'. This does not work! You will only gain skills in birdwatching by having the goods to hand, and by using them all the time. Practise your 'quick-draw' skills on the garden birds: keep your eyes on the bird, and bring the binoculars between eyes and bird. In the second or so that this takes, make a mental note of the immediate surroundings of the bird, for instance the arrangement of twigs, so that when the binoculars are in place you quickly home in on the bird. All this will become second nature – but only if you practise it! Between uses, keep the binoculars focussed in the middle distance, so that when you locate a bird, you will have only a minimal movement of the adjustment to focus.

If you are just starting out birdwatching, you may well be baffled by the variety of binoculars for sale - and the variety of claims for them. The specifications in the form '8×40' tell you that the binoculars magnify by eight times, and that the diameter of the objective lenses – the big lenses – is 40 mm. The wider the lenses, the brighter the view (other considerations being equal), the down-side being that the bigger the objective lenses, the heavier and more cumbersome the binoculars will be.

Do not be fooled into buying anything with a magnification higher than 10×: such binoculars inevitably have a narrow field of view (so finding birds through them is tricky), the picture will not be bright (and actually dull in the poor light of dusk and winter), and worst of all, when hand-held, any slight tremble is greatly magnified. Although many dedicated birdwatchers have binoculars with magnifications of up to 10×, we recommend 6× to 8× magnification. These will be easy to handle, will have bright wide-angle views with little tremble, and can be light-weight.

As far as cost is concerned, you will get what you pay for, up to a point. The very finest binoculars will be fully waterproof, robust, crystal-clear, and possibly so heavy that your neck may be feeling the strain by the end of the day, and so expensive that you'll be tempted to leave them in safety at home. Much better to have something that you will take out and use: if you're worrying all the time about keeping them safe, you'll not enjoy them, nor the birding. Most of the time, the more ordinary binoculars will serve you well. Some of the modern compact binoculars, with specifications such as 8×23, are very impressive, and perfect for comfortable use, only letting you down in the late dusk when light really begins to fail.

Light and compact binoculars may thus serve you better on walks than heavy and cumbersome ones. If you still find them neck-straining, try the wide neoprene straps which work well to spread the load. Or simply run a cord from the back of the strap down to a belt at your waist: this will take the strain off your neck onto your shoulders, and is handy enough if you rig up a clip of some sort for either or both ends. Usually with new binoculars you will need to shorten the strap, perhaps a great deal. See where other people wear theirs, and try different lengths until you find the right length for you; mid-chest is about right.

Most modern binoculars have a central adjustment which alters the focussing for both eyes equally, and also a rotating right eye-piece which allows separate focussing for your right eye. Some users never get to grips with this arrangement! With new binoculars, cover the right-hand objective lens completely, for example with the lens-cap, and focus on a middle-distance object with the central adjustment, and using only your left eye. Now cover the left lens, and focus for your right eye with the rotating right eye-piece. Keep both eyes open during this exercise: your eyes must be relaxed. With both eyes in use, the two views should both be perfectly focussed. Make a note of the plus or minus setting on the eye-piece, and check the adjustment often - it tends to drift off the correct setting for your eyes.

Many binoculars have rubber eye-cups which bend back to allow spectacle-wearers to view through their spectacles. If you find that this restricts your view unacceptably, practise lifting the spectacles with one hand and the binoculars with the other. The spectacles can then rest on the top of the binoculars. This sounds clumsy, but with practice can be a better option. One of the authors has used it for twenty-five years! Spectacles on a cord is another option. However, if your defect is anything other than simple long- or short-sight, you may need the spectacles as well.

There are some superb second-hand bargains possible from reputable dealers, but make sure binoculars are not 'discollimated': the two separate views you get through them with your two eyes must coincide perfectly. If they do not, the prisms may be misaligned.

Terrestrial telescopes

You may find a telescope and tripod a real boon, especially on the estuary or lake walks. Many birdwatchers carry them for much of the time. They tend, however, to be both heavy and cumbersome for use on a longer walk. You can get light-weight combinations, although these will inevitably be less steady in use than heavier ones. One of the authors has a 'spotting-scope'/tripod combination weighing just 2.5 kg. A monopod is much lighter, but hardly steady enough, and you will rarely find a suitable place to rest a telescope if you try to do without a tripod.

Look for an objective lens of 60 mm and a magnification of about 30×. The zoom lenses available for some models can be useful, but in general have a much narrower field of view. Magnifications of 50× or 60× can be useful when conditions are ideal, but the telescope mount must be very steady, and heat-shimmer which is hardly noticeable to the unaided eye can render an image at 60× entirely useless!

Identification

You will need a good field-guide for the British Isles. If you are just beginning, perhaps avoid for the moment the comprehensive guides for larger areas, such as for the whole of Europe, or Europe plus North Africa. You will need one of those if you are going abroad, but for starting out in the UK, the sheer profusion of species is likely to confuse rather than illuminate, and you will find yourself considering all sorts of species which do not occur here, or are only rare strays. There are a number of excellent guides which deal first of all with the more likely species (which can include rarer birds readily seen at certain reserves, such as Osprey and Avocet).

All the birds named in our walks have been seen in the places named. In the richest areas, we have had space to mention only the more typical or special birds. Whether you find the same birds, or a different selection, will depend upon skill, timing, weather, and luck. Use the Occurrence Table to check the likelihood of your identifications. Always bear in mind that an 'odd' bird is much more likely to be a common species in an unfamiliar plumage, posture or light, than some rarity.

Bird populations are constantly changing, and it must be said that many once familiar birds are suffering declines to the extent of local extinction, especially those of intensively-managed farmland, which – although covering such large areas – is no longer a welcoming place for birds, nor indeed for other wild-life. On the positive side, a few species are increasing their Cumbrian range, and can be expected to crop up in new areas.

Some handy hints

Many groups of walkers seem habitually to travel with only limited awareness of their surroundings, in self-absorbed and noisy conversation. Such groups create an apparently bird-less zone for many yards around them: birds will fall silent, dive into cover, or slip away unseen. To find birds – beyond the most obvious ones – your attention must be focussed outwards. The larger your group, the more difficult this is to maintain! To locate the most birds you must move quietly and steadily, pausing at intervals to allow the shyer ones to relax and perhaps emerge from cover, and scanning wider views for any which might take flight as you approach.

Early morning is usually the most productive time to watch birds.

Some birds are elusive or retiring; others, while not shy, live in dense cover from which they seldom emerge. For all these, the songs and calls are the usual means of detection. There are many species mentioned in our walks to which this applies – warblers being obvious examples – but even for such 'visible' species as thrushes and tits you will locate – and with practice identify – many more by song or call than you will ever catch sight of.

For some flighty birds, the calls again provide certain identification. Linnets, Redpolls and Siskins flying overhead as tiny silhouettes can be readily separated by call, as can geese and many waders, flying at too great a distance for visual identification, or in conditions of mist or poor light.

Getting familiar with the songs and calls of birds takes concentration, time and patience, and some human ears or brains seem more adept than others. The only solution is to follow up unfamiliar calls and songs, and identify the originator. You may find that learning from the many excellent tapes and CDs now available helps. With the advent of portable CD and minidisk players, it is possible to check a recording of the species against the bird in the field.

July and August are popular months for visiting Cumbria, but it must be said that although there are numbers of birds present in most habitats in high summer, it can be difficult to locate those which are silent, and perhaps in moult – during which all birds keep a low profile. Most woodland species stop singing promptly in early July, and from being noisy and evidently teeming with birds in the height of the song-period in April and May, suddenly the woods can seem dead and empty. Birds such as tits gather into a few roving flocks, so – depending on your luck – you may see many, or none.

Things pick up somewhat towards September, and from then onwards, many birds are actively migrating. Summer residents move south, passage migrants move through, and winter migrants arrive. A prodigious exchange of birds is taking place, in numbers which are difficult to comprehend, the migration of most species being largely hidden from human eyes.

Although far fewer birds over-winter in Cumbrian inland habitats than spend the summer, by way of recompense there are huge numbers – and good variety – in many coastal areas. Such changes are also reflected in our walks. Many of the inland and especially upland walks will be most rewarding in spring and summer, but less so in winter. Conversely, at that time, many of the coastal walks are at their most interesting.

Disclaimer

Whilst every effort has been made to represent the route accurately in the route description, neither the authors nor the publisher can accept any responsibility in connection with any trespass arising from the use of the definitive route or any associated route.

Whilst the authors have walked and researched the routes for the purpose of this guide, no responsibility can be accepted for any unforeseen circumstances encountered while following them.

South Walney

Start: Biggar Bank car-park **Grid ref:** SD184664 **Distance:** 8 miles/13 km
Maps: Landranger Sheet 96; Outdoor Leisure 6 *English Lakes (SW)*

This walk provides wonderful birdwatching all year round and the opportunity to become familiar with the waders of Morecambe Bay. Flocks of roosting birds consist typically of Oystercatcher, Curlew, Redshank, Dunlin, Turnstone, Knot, Ringed Plover and Grey Plover. To make the most of it, ensure you consult tide tables: the whole coastline is excellent at any high tide over 9 metres, but pay particular attention to the shingle spits on the east side, the refuse tip on the west and South Walney Nature Reserve with its six birdwatching hides.

1 Bent Haw has roosting waders with the bonus of a Walney winter speciality, Purple Sandpiper (between October and March).

2 Hillock Whins – wader roost. In spring-time, watch out for migrant birds such as Wheatear, Whinchat and Sedge Warbler. The gorse bushes and hedgerows hold Stonechat and Linnet while the low-lying fields support small gatherings of Whimbrel (first two weeks of May).

3 Refuse Tip – wader/gull roost. Diligent scrutiny of the gull roost in winter and spring may provide sightings of Glaucous and Iceland Gull. Hooded Crows are regular with the numerous other corvids. Autumn and winter produce mixed finch flocks, including Twite.

4 South Walney Nature Reserve (obtain day permit from kiosk) – waders, wildfowl and gulls. The spring-time spectacle of thousands of nesting gulls is exhilarating – but wear old clothes! – the area is home also to Britain's most southerly Eider colony. Other breeding birds include Shelduck, Ringed Plover, Oystercatcher, Sandwich, Little, Common and Arctic Tern. The hides are a boon for visiting birdwatchers. Seawatching in spring and autumn yields Gannet, Manx Shearwater, Great and Arctic Skua, Kittiwake, Guillemot and Razorbill, while Red-throated Diver and Common Scoter can be seen in winter. The spit, gravel pools, Lighthouse Bay and Walney Channel are havens for Little and Great Crested Grebe, Mallard, Wigeon, Teal, Shoveler, Pintail, Shelduck, Red-breasted Merganser and Cormorant. In autumn especially, look out for Greenshank on the pools. Search the bushes; South Walney is a magnet for migrant birds and anything may turn up.

5 Scar End Point – wader roost. This shingle headland holds Lapwing, Golden Plover and Bar-tailed Godwit. Raptors (Merlin, Peregrine and Sparrowhawk) are regularly seen pursuing waders.

6 Snab Point is an excellent wildfowl viewing location and the whins attract migrants in spring and autumn.

7 Wylock Marsh – waders, wildfowl and gulls. In winter this locality teems with Shelduck, Mallard, Wigeon, Pintail, Lapwing, Redshank and Skylark.

8 Long Rein Point – waders and wildfowl. Another superb viewpoint with the possibility of migrant birds utilising the hedgerows.

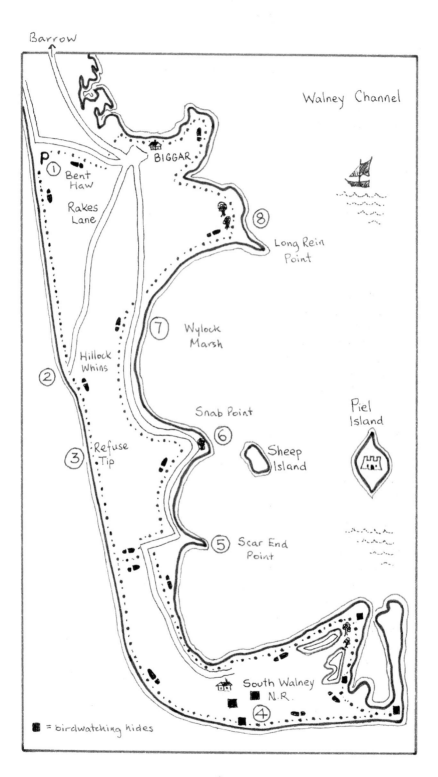

Barrow

Walney Channel

P ①
Bent Haw

Rakes Lane

BIGGAR

⑧
Long Rein Point

⑦
Wylock Marsh

Hillock Whins

②

Snab Point

⑥

Piel Island

③
Refuse Tip

Sheep Island

⑤ Scar End Point

South Walney N.R.

④

■ = birdwatching hides

Cavendish Dock & Rampside

Start: St George the Martyr Church   **Grid ref:** SD203693   **Distance:** 6 miles/10 km

Maps: Landranger Sheet 96; Outdoor Leisure 6 *English Lakes (SW)*

Spectacular numbers of wildfowl and waders are guaranteed for most of the year providing your walk coincides with a tide of 9 metres. An eye-opening stroll from St George the Martyr church along Cavendish Dock Road leads to the dock itself, one of the northwest's premier wildfowl havens.

1   A first glimpse of the dock from behind the shelter of the wall can produce close views of Little and Great Crested Grebe, Cormorant, Mute Swan, Mallard, Wigeon, Pochard, Tufted Duck, Goldeneye, Red-breasted Merganser and Coot.

2   From the southwest corner, the whole panorama of the dock is spread before you. Diligent watching especially in winter may reveal some of the site's speciality birds which include Red-throated, Black-throated and Great Northern Divers, Black-necked, Red-necked and Slavonian Grebes, Scaup, Long-tailed Duck and Ruddy Duck. The 'wall' in mid-dock holds large numbers of Cormorant and at high tide roosting Redshank and Dunlin. Little Gull and Black Tern have been seen in spring and Stonechat is resident.

3   The causeway walk provides fine views of innumerable waders and ducks, notably Oystercatcher, Lapwing, Golden Plover, Curlew, Redshank, Dunlin, Knot, Wigeon and Shelduck. Look out for Rock Pipit (winter), Common Sandpiper and White Wagtail (spring) and Grey Wagtail (autumn). Peregrine and Merlin hunt the mudflats.

4   The reedy area holds Teal, Snipe and Water Rail in winter, but patience is needed. Chaffinch, Goldfinch, Greenfinch, Meadow Pipit and Reed Bunting can be found foraging along the tideline.

5   The walk to Westfield Point produces large gatherings of feeding waders and wildfowl especially if this section of the route coincides with the outgoing tide. The shrubs and bushes alongside the terminal hold migrants in spring and autumn.

6   Ridding Head Scar – waders and wildfowl. Often Bar-tailed Godwit and Golden Plover are to be seen in winter. Eiders are evident throughout the year and Ringed Plover breed on the beach.

7   The gorse and bracken on the cliffs are home to Linnet and Stonechat.

8   Greylag Geese, Mute Swan, Coot, Moorhen and Reed Bunting breed on the small pool while to the south, the hedgerows shelter migrants in spring and autumn.

9   Winter flocks of waders and wildfowl plus a Rampside speciality, Brent Goose (October to April), can be seen at high tide. The return walk inland follows lanes lined with hawthorns which are utilised by Fieldfare and Redwing in autumn and winter. Grey Heron is often to be seen in the low-lying fields. From the viewpoint above the Gas Terminal, the path meanders through the complex before meeting the coastal route.

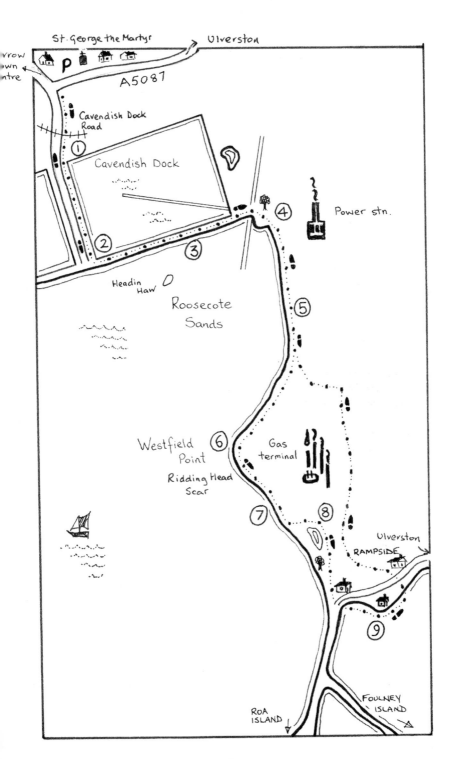

St. George the Martyr   Ulverston

Barrow Town Centre

A5087

Cavendish Dock Road

①

Cavendish Dock

②

③

④   Power stn.

Heading Haw

Roosecote Sands

⑤

Westfield Point

⑥   Gas terminal

Ridding Head Scar

⑦   ⑧

Ulverston

RAMPSIDE

⑨

ROA ISLAND

FOULNEY ISLAND

Sandscale & the Duddon Estuary

Start: Park Road   **Grid ref:** SD199736   **Distance:** 7 miles/11 km
Maps: Landranger Sheet 96; Outdoor Leisure 6 *English Lakes (SW)*

There are a number of sites that hold good quantities of waders so consult tide tables for 9 metre tides. However, high tides don't always matter; even at low tide you'll see plenty of birds feeding on the mud flats. Watch out for birds of prey, especially Merlin, Peregrine and Short-eared Owl.

1 In autumn, the copse near the main road supports a tit flock; Redpoll, Siskin and Goldcrest have all been recorded here, as has Black Redstart among the gaunt industrial remains.

2 Scarth Bight has Shelduck, Lapwing and Redshank in high numbers for most of the year. Grey Heron is often to be seen. In summer you'll see Sandwich Terns fishing and groups of Eider ducks with their ducklings. Winter brings Goldeneye, Red-breasted Merganser and Cormorant.

3 The wet meadow is very productive in winter. Mallard, Teal and Wigeon are guaranteed, and maybe Shoveler. Hen Harrier is a distinct possibility. In spring you may not see, but certainly should hear, Sedge Warbler. During summer, the dunes are alive with Skylark and Meadow Pipit and you should witness displaying Snipe, Lapwing and Redshank. The area is home to the scarce Natterjack Toad whose far-carrying 'song' can best be heard on calm, warm nights in May and June. In these months look out for Cuckoo and Stonechat on the stunted hawthorn bushes.

4 Roanhead Crag – wader and gull roost. High tide in winter yields Oystercatcher, Lapwing, Curlew, Dunlin, Knot, Grey Plover and a handful of Sanderling. It's a good venue for studying gulls with Black-headed, Common, Herring, Lesser Black-backed and Great Black-backed, all side by side and available for comparison.

5 At low tide this part of the Duddon Sands is a major feeding ground for all the area's waders and excellent views can be obtained as you approach Askam Pier. Great Crested Grebe, Goldeneye and Red-breasted Merganser are a certainty on a full tide in winter and there is always the chance of Scaup and Long-tailed Duck. Kestrel and Sparrowhawk patrol the scrub areas behind the reed bed which is itself home to Reed Bunting throughout the year and Sedge Warbler in summer. Snipe can be found in the winter, feeding or roosting in the damp patches.

6 Turnstone and Redshank congregate on Askam Pier in winter and Rock Pipit can also be seen. Breathtaking views of waders and wildfowl can be had from the end of the pier as the birds leave their roosts for the first exposed mud flats of the Duddon. The saltmarsh to the north holds plenty of Redshank while Dunlin flocks can be found on the mud as the tide recedes. Even the Askam cliffs are worth a look at high tide; often you will see small groups of Ringed Plover and Turnstone.

7 The wader roost at Lowsy Point holds Oystercatcher, Curlew, Dunlin and perhaps Bar-tailed Godwit.

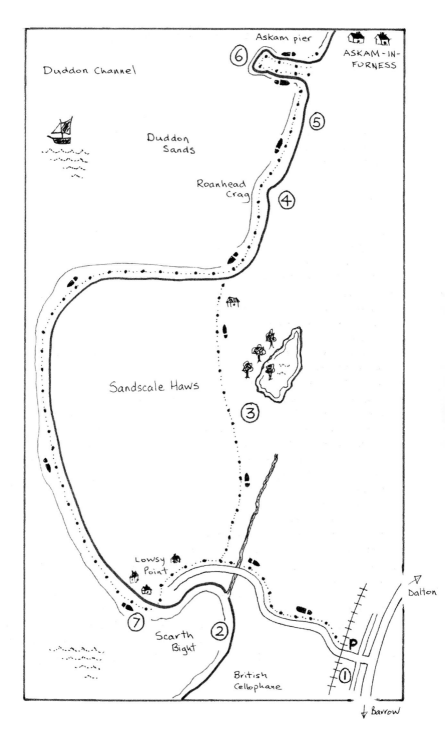

Duddon Channel

Askam pier

ASKAM-IN-
FURNESS

⑥

⑤

Duddon
Sands

Roanhead
Crag

④

Sandscale Haws

③

Lowsy
Point

⑦

Scarth
Bight

②

British
Cellophane

Dalton

P

①

↓ Barrow

II

Askam-in-Furness & Sand Side

Start: Beach Road, Askam   **Grid ref:** SD210781   **Distance:** 7 miles/11 km
Maps: Landranger Sheet 96; Outdoor Leisure 6 *English Lakes (SW)*

As with all estuary walks a 9 metre tide provides the best birdwatching proposition. There are outstanding opportunities to view waders and wildfowl and the Duddon is a particularly good site for Sanderling and Pintail, two species with a limited distribution within the county. Aim to be on the top of the limestone outcrop at Dunnerholme for high tide. From this superb vantage point, estuary bird movements can be witnessed in front of a tremendously scenic Lake District backdrop, arguably the most spectacular birdwatching site in Cumbria.

1 Winter viewing from the car-park yields a variety of waders most usually Oyster-catcher, Lapwing, Redshank, Curlew and Grey Plover along with ducks such as Mallard and Shelduck. Out in mid-channel Great Crested Grebe and small groups of Eider, Goldeneye and Red-breasted Merganser should be seen. The cliff top fence posts are perches for Stonechat, while Goldfinch, Linnet and Greenfinch are also regular.

2 The outfall, spilling onto the sands, attracts a wide variety of species. Waders such as Lapwing, Grey Plover, Dunlin, Redshank and Oystercatcher can be seen out on the mud flats, while there are Mallard, Black-headed and Common Gull closer to the beach.

3 The wide expanse that spreads north to Dunnerholme accommodates a substantial Ringed Plover roost – motionless, they look remarkably like stones! The activity along the edge of the incoming tide never ceases with Dunlin, Knot, Grey Plover, Redshank and Sanderling all feeding frantically.

4 Dunnerholme – wader and wildfowl roost. The sands to the north are dominated by large assemblies of Oystercatcher, Lapwing and Curlew. Bar-tailed Godwit are often mixed in with the Curlew. In the distance, Pintail flocks, together with a few Wigeon and Teal, can be seen. Peregrine and Merlin are daily in winter – check the tops of fence posts. Great Crested Grebe, Red-breasted Merganser, Goldeneye and Scaup can be located in mid-channel. Migrants, most usually Redwing and Fieldfare, utilise the hawthorns on the north side of the rock. The walk from Dunnerholme to Sand Side meanders through rushes and across sea-washed turf. Meadow Pipit, Skylark, Reed Bunting and Snipe are all likely, and there is always the possibility of Short-eared Owl.

5 Sand Side Marsh has concentrations of wildfowl throughout the winter with Pintail and Shelduck usually the most numerous species. Mallard, Wigeon and Teal will be seen in smaller numbers and geese, either Greylag or Pink-footed, are often across the water on Angerton Marsh.

6 After passing the Sand Side rookery, the small copse at the top of the hill is well worth a stop with both Great Spotted Woodpecker and Treecreeper regular visitors.

7 Soutergate Beck supports Dipper and Grey Wagtail.

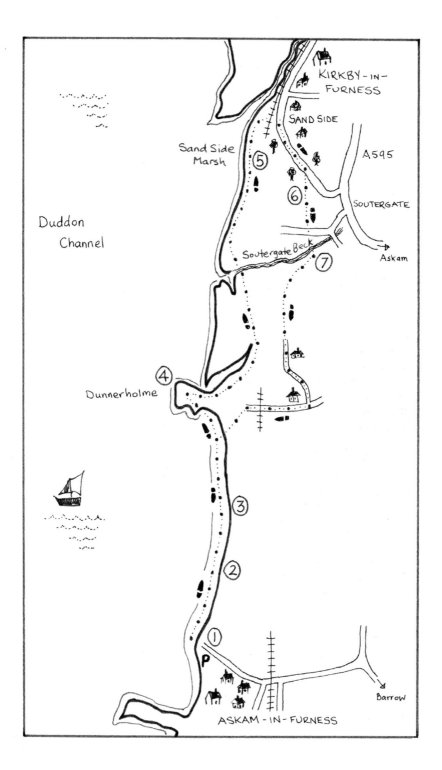

Duddon
Channel

KIRKBY-IN-
FURNESS

SAND SIDE

Sand Side
Marsh

⑤

A595

⑥

SOUTERGATE

Soutergate Beck

⑦

Askam

④

Dunnerholme

③

②

①

P

ASKAM-IN-FURNESS

Barrow

Lickle Valley

Start: Bank End   **Grid ref:** SD199883   **Distance:** 6 miles/10 km
Maps: Landranger Sheet 96; Outdoor Leisure 6 *English Lakes (SW)*

The River Lickle rises to the east of Caw and tumbles for two miles before being joined by the Appletree Worth Beck. For the next five miles, until it reaches the Duddon Estuary, the river passes through one of the prettiest and least populated valleys in southwest Cumbria. The birdwatcher is well catered for with woodland, moorland and riverside species and an abundance of Buzzards, most obvious on sunny days in spring.

1   Usually, soaring Buzzards can be seen from the lay-by at Bank End. The uphill stretch to Glade Haw passes scrub and deciduous woodland, the haunt of Great, Blue, Coal, Marsh and Long-tailed Tits. Goldcrest, Treecreeper, Great Spotted Woodpecker, Buzzard and Mistle Thrush nest among the Scots Pine trees.

2   The path's altitude offers expansive views. The low-lying fields produce Greylag Geese, Grey Heron and Mallard. A small heronry is visible in the larch plantation across the valley. The ox-bows of the river are favoured haunts of Teal and Goosander. Look out for Roe Deer and Pheasants in the scrubland bordering the fields. Goldcrest is regular in the conifers behind Lower Bleansley.

3   The open parkland type of habitat to the east of the road affords glimpses of Jay and Green Woodpecker, while to the west, a larch plantation is home to Buzzard, migrating Fieldfare and Redwing. Finches, usually Chaffinch and Goldfinch, can be found foraging in the fields either side of the road.

4   The route climbs steeply between deciduous woodland to Hawes. The National Trust property has a well-stocked bird table and is a rendezvous for woodland birds which include Great Spotted Woodpecker and hunting Sparrowhawks. Siskin are not infrequent and it is also a venue for small numbers of Yellowhammer, which forsake the open moorland in winter.

5   Among the bracken beneath Great Stickle are Wren and Meadow Pipit. Whinchat breed here in summer and 'kronk'-ing Ravens tumble out of the skies. Peregrine, Merlin and Kestrel have all been recorded here. The rushy area near the cruck barn harbours Snipe.

6   The path descends between oak and birch woods which hold migratory Redwing and Fieldfare and resident Mistle Thrushes and Green Woodpecker. The bridge over the River Lickle is a good vantage point for Dipper and Grey Wagtail as is the old mill just south of Broughton Mills.

7   The hedgerows bordering the river are utilised by Long-tailed Tit and Reed Bunting. The southward path along the valley affords constant opportunities to watch 'sky-dancing' Buzzards in spring.

8   Viewing from the bridge over the River Lickle just west of Middle Bleansley offers the possibility of Grey Wagtail, Dipper, Goosander, Mallard and Teal. Snipe can be located in the damper parts of the fields.

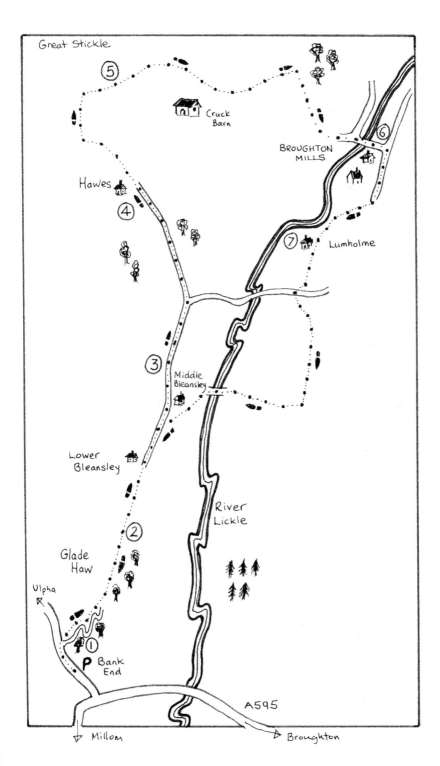

Great Stickle

⑤

Cruck
Barn

BROUGHTON
MILLS

⑥

Hawes

④

⑦ Lumholme

③ Middle
Bleansley

Lower
Bleansley

River
Lickle

②

Glade
Haw

Ulpha

①

P Bank
End

A595

Millom

Broughton

15

Millom & the Duddon Estuary

Start: Lancashire Road   **Grid ref:** SD175804   **Distance:** 7½ miles/12 km
Maps: Landranger Sheet 96; Outdoor Leisure 6 *English Lakes (SW)*

This walk along the western side of the Duddon Estuary offers excellent close range views of winter wildfowl and waders. A tide of 9 metres is absolutely essential for birdwatching Millom Marsh; anything less means that the high tide roosts are less concentrated and at least half a mile away out on the saltmarsh. Additionally, conifer-dominated Millom Park is well worth a leisurely perusal at any time of the year.

1 At the northern end of Lancashire Road, the embankment path skirts the saltmarsh and heads north. For its whole length you will be entertained by the quantity and quality of the Duddon birds. The Borwick Rails slag bank which juts out into the estuary effectively creates a bay of the southern end into which are funnelled shelter-seeking waders, wildfowl and gulls. Mallard, Wigeon, Teal, Pintail and Shelduck are joined by Oystercatcher, Redshank and Curlew. Take particular note of the 'small brown jobs' on the sea-washed turf; Meadow Pipit, Skylark, Rock Pipit, Linnet and Twite are all regular here in winter. Wader roosts are a feature of the embankment walk; in among the Curlew, Redshank and Oystercatcher are small numbers of Bar-tailed Godwit, while Dunlin can be seen in impressive flocks. Snipe can often be flushed from the ditch to the west. Out in the channel are Cormorants, Great Crested Grebe, Goldeneye and Red-breasted Merganser. Both Common and Grey Seal have been seen well up the estuary in recent years. In winter, Rock Pipits are to be seen throughout the length of the embankment, while Reed Bunting should be looked for, perched atop bushes. Grey Heron, Greylag and Pink-footed Geese utilise the fields.

2 In autumn and winter, the vegetable field to the west of Green Road station usually holds Chaffinch, Greenfinch, Goldfinch and with luck Tree Sparrow.

3 Dipper and Goosander can be seen from the bridge over Black Beck, and the riverside trees are visited by parties of Long-tailed Tits.

4 The undulating country between Dunningwell and Millom Park holds resident Buzzard, Green Woodpecker and winter thrushes. Listen for spring Chiffchaffs and summer Blackcaps in the Dunningwell woodland. In early summer look for Yellowhammer in the gorse bushes and Willow Warbler at the edge of woodland.

5 Millom Park is almost exclusively dominated by conifers. Goldcrest and Coal Tit can be seen throughout the year, while during summer, the area near Park House has breeding Willow Warbler, Whitethroat, Redpoll, Sparrowhawk and roding Woodcock. A flock of Yellowhammers is regular in winter. Teal frequent the small pool at the southern end of the plantation; the adjacent pine is a perch for a resident Buzzard. Crossbill flocks can be a feature of winter; look for them in Norway spruce trees. Emerging from Millom Park, clear days can provide tremendous views of the Irish Sea coasts.

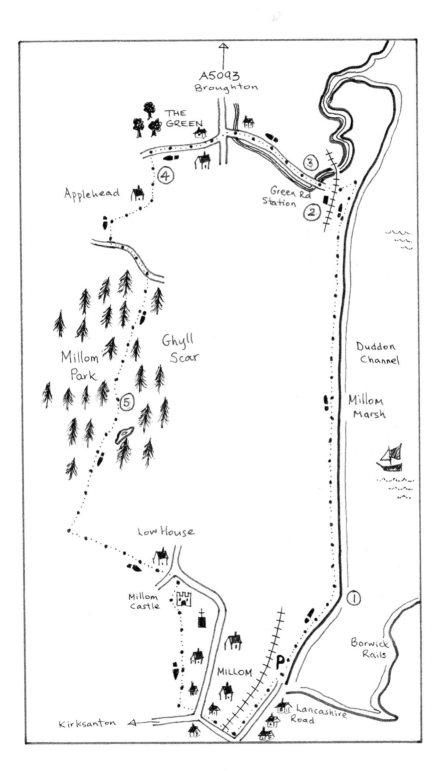

Whitbeck & Bootle

Start: A595, Whitbeck   **Grid ref:** SD119839   **Distance:** 6 miles/10 km
Maps: Landranger Sheet 96; Outdoor Leisure 6 *English Lakes (SW)*

This walk is a microcosm of all that is best for the birdwatcher in the county. There
are a variety of habitats including wetland willow scrub, boulder strewn coast, a tidal
river, a reed fringed tarn and moorland.

1 The lane that leads from Whitbeck to Gutterby takes you through farmland and
past the willow scrub bordering the Mosses. Huge flocks of Carrion Crows, Jackdaws
and Rooks are a feature of the fields and Buzzards can often be located on fence-posts
or the electricity pylons. Around the willows Long-tailed Tits are common and in
autumn the bushes can be alive with finches and Yellowhammers, the mixed flocks
providing prey for Sparrowhawks. Watch out too for Redwings and Fieldfares in
winter. The fields should be searched for grazing geese, most likely to be Greylags,
and it is always well worth glancing back towards Black Combe for tantalising
glimpses of raptors such as Kestrel and Buzzard patrolling the hillside. Nearer the
beach is a regular site for Little Owl, Goldfinch and Linnet.

2 The cliffs above Gutterby are patrolled by Buzzard and Kestrel. Scan the beach for
Turnstone, Oystercatcher, Curlew and Ringed Plover. Winter and spring may provide
views of offshore Red-throated Divers and Red-breasted Mergansers, while in summer
Gannets can be seen.

3 The cliff top path holds Meadow Pipit, Skylark, Stonechat, Wheatear, Linnet and
in winter, possibly Twite.

4 The walk up the River Annas can usually be relied upon to produce Grey Heron,
Goosander, Lapwing, Curlew, Snipe, Common Gull, and Dipper. The area is also
a hunting ground for Barn Owl. Look out for the vast quantities of the snail *Helix
aspersa* which congregate underneath the railway bridge.

5 Barfield Tarn can be viewed from the public footpath. Birds seen here will include
Grey Heron, Mallard, Tufted Duck, Pochard, Goldeneye, Goosander, Moorhen,
Coot, Sedge Warbler and Reed Bunting. Osprey has been recorded from here both
in spring and autumn and the area provides ample feeding opportunities for migrating
Swallow, House Martin and Sand Martin.

6 The southward walk along the side of Black Combe offers an unparalleled chance
to see four species of raptor: Buzzard, Kestrel, Peregrine and Merlin. Spring-time is
probably the optimum time for viewing, but mid-summer, when young birds have
fledged, can be just as spectacular. Yellowhammer, Linnet, Stonechat and Whinchat
are all likely in summer, and Goldcrest can often be seen in autumn around Fell
Cottage.

7 The lush hedgerows around the hamlet of Whitbeck are haunts for all the commoner
garden birds and in addition may produce Blackcap, Willow Warbler, Goldcrest
and Siskin, the latter especially in the autumn.

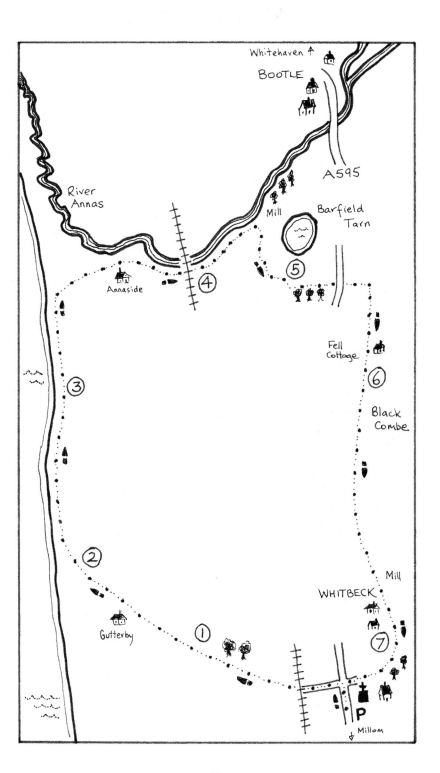

Whitehaven ↑

BOOTLE

A595

River
Annas

Mill

Barfield
Tarn

④

⑤

Annaside

Fell
Cottage

③

⑥

Black
Combe

②

Mill

WHITBECK

①

Gutterby

⑦

P

↓ Millom

Muncaster & Ravenglass

Start: Ravenglass   **Grid ref:** SD085964   **Distance:** 6 miles/10 km
Maps: Landranger Sheet 96; Outdoor Leisure 6 *English Lakes (SW)*

It is absolutely paramount that tide tables are consulted for this walk. The coastal stretch south of Ravenglass can only be walked at low tide. At high tide the route is impassable and consequently extremely dangerous.

1 The confluence of the Rivers Esk, Mite and Irt provides rich feeding grounds for a variety of birds. This activity is best seen at low tide when the creeks and channels are haunts for Cormorant and a variety of ducks, waders and gulls. Redshank and Oystercatcher are the commonest waders but you should also see Curlew and Turnstone. Less regular waders include both Grey Plover and, especially in autumn, Greenshank. Wigeon and Red-breasted Merganser frequent the estuary, the former quite numerous in winter, when it is also possible to see small numbers of Goldeneye. The embankment bushes bordering the railway line often support Long-tailed Tit.

2 The saltmarsh to the east of the railway bridge is a gathering site for Teal, Wigeon and Mallard. Flocks of Chaffinch, Linnet and maybe Brambling utilise the hawthorn hedgerows in winter and the fields to the north can hold a flock of Stock Dove. Look out for Greylag Geese on the south side of the estuary and Buzzard patrolling for carrion.

3 The woodland to the north of the Cumbria Coastal Way holds Great Spotted Woodpecker, Long-tailed Tit, and in autumn, Goldcrest.

4 Yellowhammer can be located on the gorse covered crag and Buzzard is regularly recorded surveying the open areas.

5 The small plantation and large deciduous trees to the north of Newtown can be productive with resident Bullfinch, Great Spotted Woodpecker, Green Woodpecker and Treecreeper.

6 At the path into Muncaster Castle woods, a fine view of the estuary can be had before a steeply descending track takes you into an exquisite woodland. Here you can be sure of Coal Tit, Treecreeper and Nuthatch before emerging into the castle complex and its fine collection of exotic wildfowl and owls. Muncaster churchyard is another regular site for Nuthatch and in winter you should see both Siskin and Redpoll, while in summer, Spotted Flycatcher can be observed.

7 The track to the north of the A595 supports Willow Warbler, Chiffchaff, Blackcap, Garden Warbler, Whitethroat and Wood Warbler in summer, while in winter, roving bands of tits and Goldcrests are met with. Roe Deer, too, can often be observed.

8 The track to the south of the A595 leads through more woodland, another haunt for summer-time warblers and winter-time tits.

9 Dunlin, Redshank and Curlew probe the low tide mud near the railway bridge at Ravenglass.

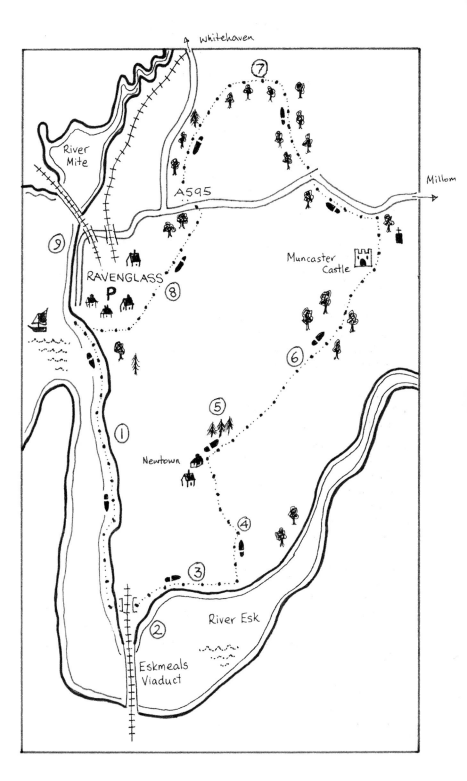

Gosforth & Nether Wasdale

Start: Wellington Bridge   **Grid ref:** NY079040 **Distance:** 8 miles/13 km
Maps: Landranger Sheet 89; Outdoor Leisure 6 *English Lakes (SW)*

Western Lakeland is very much under-birdwatched. What birdwatching is done tends to be concentrated on the coast. Inland there are fine river ways which are migration routes and specialised breeding areas. This particular walk incorporates the rivers Bleng and Irt in their upper reaches, moorland and both deciduous and coniferous woodland. Stop in Gosforth and visit St Mary the Virgin church with its 10th century cross and Norse hogback tombstones.

1 Wellington Bridge and the road alongside the Bleng provides a suitable vantage point to see Dipper, Grey Wagtail, Pied Wagtail and possibly Goosander.

2 The bridleway that strikes northeast up to Hollow Moor has hedgerows that in some winters are full of Fieldfare and Redwing. The path provides fine views across to Blengdale Forest; Buzzard and Sparrowhawk may be seen displaying and patrolling.

3 The route from Between Guards and Guards Head is a site for Little Owl, Stonechat and Yellowhammer. The conifers of Hollow Moor are home to Long-eared Owl, Sparrowhawk, Coal Tit and Goldcrest. In winter, small parties of Redpoll and Siskin, and occasionally Crossbill have been recorded.

4 Spectacular views into Wast Water and across to the Screes provide opportunities to see Raven, Kestrel and Peregrine. The little woodland at Yew Tree holds Mistle Thrush, Chaffinch and Goldcrest and in winter Fieldfare, Redwing and Brambling may be encountered.

5 Small separated woods are good sites to watch. The numerous deciduous woods along the route to Nether Wasdale are no exception and both Green Woodpecker and Great Spotted Woodpecker can often best be seen as their bounding flight carries them across the gaps between the woodlands.

6 Jackdaws are ever present in Nether Wasdale, and the village with its superb backdrop is over-flown by Raven, Buzzard and Peregrine, and at one time, and may still be, and hopefully will be, by Golden Eagle.

7 Birks Wood and Foxbield Wood produce Great Spotted Woodpecker, Tawny Owl and Jay throughout the year. Additionally, the Nuthatch, which has been increasing its distribution in Cumbria at an amazing rate in the last twenty years, has spread to these woods. Summer-time sees Chiffchaff, Blackcap, Garden and Willow Warbler, Redstart, Spotted Flycatcher and Pied Flycatcher.

8 Both Gaterigghow Bridge and Hallbolton Bridge are good sites to view Dipper, Grey Wagtail and Goosander. There is also the possibility of Common Sandpiper in summer.

9 The westerly walk alongside the River Bleng should provide Dipper and Grey Wagtail. Grey Partridge, very much a declining species in Britain and Cumbria, has been recorded on numerous occasions in the low-lying fields to the west of the track.

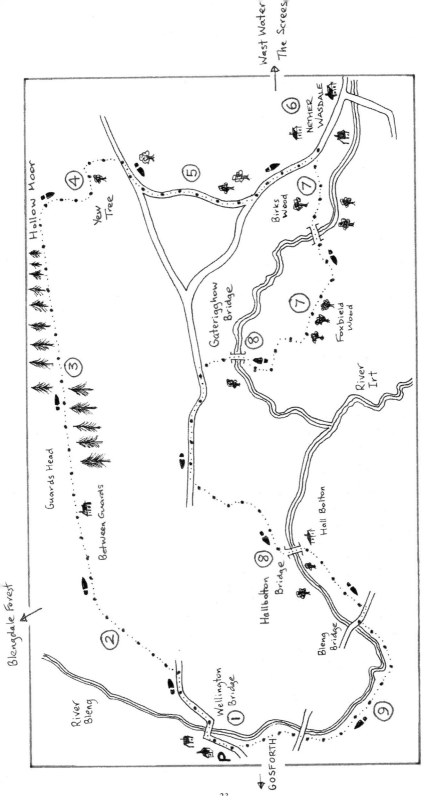

Blengdale Forest

River Bleng

Guards Head

Hollow Moor

Wast Water
The Screes

Yew Tree

Between Guards

Gaterigghow Bridge

Birks Wood

NETHER WASDALE

Foxbield Wood

River Irt

Hall Bolton

Hallbolton Bridge

Bleng Bridge

Wellington Bridge

GOSFORTH

① ② ③ ④ ⑤ ⑥ ⑦ ⑦ ⑧ ⑧ ⑨

P

23

St Bees Head

Start: St Bees seafront   **Grid ref:** NX961118   **Distance:** 6½ miles/10.5 km
Maps: Landranger Sheet 89; Pathfinder Sheet 593

Within Cumbria the imposing red sandstone cliffs of St Bees Head provide a unique habitat. It is an RSPB reserve and the eroded ledges are nesting sites for some of the most exciting seabirds in Britain. A visit in June, at the height of the breeding season, will offer a spectacular insight into the lives of the inhabitants of this seabird city. As an added bonus, the visit will be enhanced by the equally spectacular plant-life; the cliffs are bedecked with Thrift, Scurvy Grass, Sea Campion, and Ladies Finger and you are likely also to meet with butterfly species such as Red Admiral or Painted Lady.

1 Looking out to sea from the beach car-park you should have distant views of both Razorbill and Guillemot. Often there are Gannets fishing, and less often, but during strong westerly winds, you may see Manx Shearwater.

2 The small iris and reed patch holds breeding Sedge Warbler.

3 As the cliff path ascends look out for Linnet on the gorse bushes, Wheatear perched on the turf and boulder walls and Meadow Pipit in the rough grass. On the rocks below you should be able to glimpse the fleeting movements of Rock Pipit.

4 At the top you are afforded your first real encounter with that master of cliff top air currents, the Fulmar. Herring Gulls nest on the tops of the crumbling stacks and at the foot of the cliffs, and you may catch sight of Cormorant. Kestrel and Peregrine breed on these cliff ledges, the former often hunting the short path sward, the latter preying on the St Bees' Rock Doves.

5 The gorse area at the head of Fleswick Bay holds Stonechat, Whitethroat and Linnet. Little Owl can often be located either sitting at the entrance to rabbit burrows or atop a fence post; dusk seems to be the optimum time.

6 Fleswick Bay is an ideal picnic stop. The finer points of Rock Pipit identification can be pursued at leisure. Black Guillemot is a near certainty, riding the waves close inshore. Be aware of consternation and hubbub among the cliff residents: their concern may be due to a passing Peregrine, Arctic Skua or Great Skua.

7 The RSPB has installed viewing areas (with barricades to prevent mishaps). All of them are well worth viewing from, each giving unsurpassable views of the denizens on the cliff ledges: Fulmar, Kittiwake, Guillemot, Razorbill and Puffin. The first four of these are easy to see from all the vantage points. The northerly look-outs are the prime sites for Puffin, and often they can be located sitting on the water. Close scrutiny of the 'ledge-fuls' of Guillemot should also reveal the variant known as 'bridled' Guillemot, individuals of which have a prominent white eye-ring and curved line running back towards the nape. If you have not bumped into Raven as yet, the area just beyond the lighthouse is usually patrolled by the resident pair.

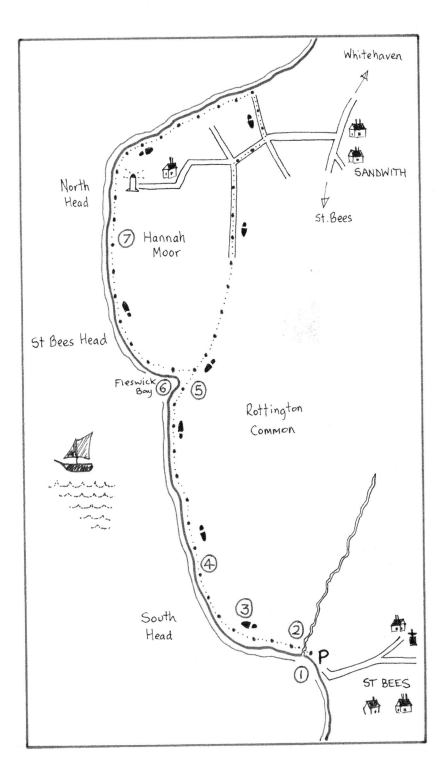

Whitehaven

SANDWITH

St. Bees

North
Head

⑦ Hannah
Moor

St Bees Head

Fleswick
Bay ⑥ ⑤

Rottington
Common

South
Head

④

③

② P

① ST BEES

Bardsea & Baycliff

Start: Wadhead Hill **Grid ref:** SD307746 **Distance:** 5 miles/8 km
Maps: Landranger Sheet 96; Outdoor Leisure 6 & 7 *English Lakes (SW & SE)*

More Morecambe Bay specialities are guaranteed on this walk in south Cumbria which incorporates mud, sand and shingle, deciduous woodland and a brief excursion on to moorland. Once again it is necessary to consult tide tables. Start your walk an hour before a 9 metre tide to ensure the best birdwatching possibilities.

1 From the car-park an expansive view across Ulverston Channel produces a variety of wildfowl, waders and gulls. Red-breasted Merganser and Eider should be seen throughout the year, while winter will yield flocks of Shelduck, Wigeon, Pintail and maybe a few Scaup. Redshank, Curlew, Lapwing and Oystercatcher are plentiful and assemblies of Ringed Plover and Dunlin can be found roosting on Wadhead Scar. Grey Heron and Cormorant fish the estuary at all times. In summer, Chapel Island provides a safe nesting site for Eider, Herring and Lesser Black-backed Gull. The trees and bushes are host to winter-time thrushes, finches and migrating passerines such as Goldcrest, Willow Warbler and Whitethroat.

2 The bridge across the beck on the north side of the A5087 is a good vantage point for Moorhen, Teal, Mallard and Reed Bunting.

3 Prior to high tide there is normally a substantial roost of Oystercatcher, Curlew, Black-headed Gull and Common Gull on Mill Scar. Bar-tailed Godwit can be encountered in small numbers throughout the length of the coast. Peregrine and Merlin hunt the estuary in autumn, winter and spring – any disturbance of the roosting waders is well worth close scrutiny.

4 All the common woodland species can be located in Sea Wood, but in addition there is the chance to see Great Spotted Woodpecker, Sparrowhawk and Nuthatch. Scan the tops of the trees: autumn can be good for migrating Siskin.

5 At Beanwell Cote, a small stream gurgles on to the beach where Grey Wagtail can often be found.

6 The lane from Baycliff to Sunbrick provides exhilarating views across Morecambe Bay and the hedgerows that line it are haunts for Redwing and Fieldfare in winter and Willow Warbler in summer. Cuckoo in summer and Green Woodpecker and Kestrel throughout the year are often to be seen in the Sea Wood area and Shelduck breed in the fields behind.

7 The buildings at Sunbrick are home to Little Owl.

8 Moorland habitat is met with on the south side of Birkrigg Common, both Yellowhammer and Linnet utilise the gorse and bracken areas, while Meadow Pipit and Skylark serenade you in spring. Dotterel has been recorded from here. Make sure you visit the stone circle, which – hidden by bracken in mid-summer – is easy to miss.

9 Hag Wood is a feeding ground for tit parties and Goldcrest in the autumn and winter. Willow Warbler is common in the summer.

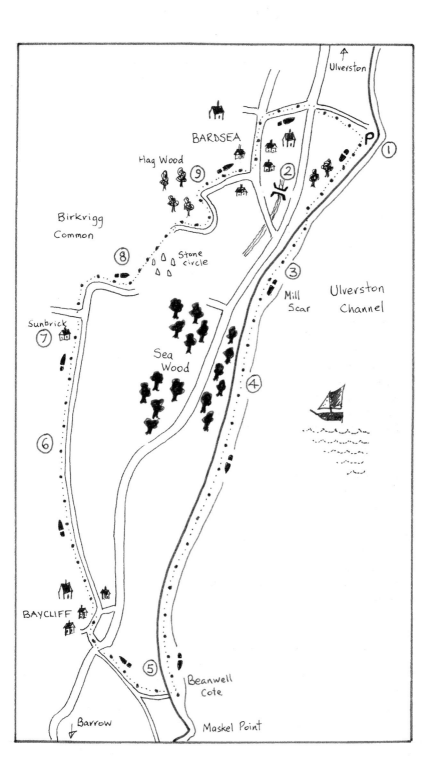

Ulverston

①

BARDSEA

Hag Wood

⑨

②

Birkrigg
Common

⑧

Stone
circle

③

Mill
Scar

Ulverston
Channel

Sunbrick

⑦

Sea
Wood

④

⑥

BAYCLIFF

⑤

Beanwell
Cote

Barrow

Maskel Point

Grizedale Forest

Start: Grizedale   **Grid ref:** SD336944   **Distance:** 5 miles/8 km
Maps: Landranger Sheet 96; Outdoor Leisure 7 *English Lakes (SE)*

This, the finest woodland locality in south Cumbria, supports healthy populations of both summer and winter visitors. At the latter time, Hawfinch can be available in impressive numbers. The more you visit Grizedale, the more it has to offer.

1 Birdwatching from the car-park can yield Grey Wagtail and Dipper on Grizedale Beck. Chaffinches are very numerous at all times and it is worth scanning the tops of the tall conifer trees for Crossbill in winter, while in summer, Pied Flycatcher utilises the many nest boxes.

2 The northward walk along the beck gives a further chance for Dipper and Grey Wagtail. Brambling in winter frequent the bridge area and all the typical woodland species, tits etc., are permanent habituées.

3 The nest boxes set among the deciduous trees hold both Pied Flycatcher and Redstart in summer and from the view point it is possible to glimpse Sparrowhawk, Great Spotted Woodpecker and even Goshawk. Goldcrest breed in the coniferous woodland.

4 The open areas of recently-felled trees provide a hunting area for Kestrel.

5 Birdwatching from the summit of Carron Crag can be exceptionally rewarding at all times of the year. Meadow Pipit can be found in the more open moorland areas, while the tops of the trees, especially in winter, hold small flocks of Redpoll, Siskin and Crossbill. Spring is the best time to witness displaying and hunting raptors such as Buzzard, Kestrel, Sparrowhawk and Goshawk, and on summer evenings, Woodcock can be seen roding.

6 The downhill walk from Carron Crag to Farra Grain Gill guarantees all the typical woodland species with the added bonus of Wood Warbler which breeds near the bridge over the gill.

7 The Farra Grain Gill valley holds Great Spotted Woodpecker, Green Woodpecker, Nuthatch and the beech trees hold a regular gathering in winter of Hawfinch. Redwing, Fieldfare and Mistle Thrush are to be found during winter among the hawthorn hedgerows and both Siskin and Redpoll can be located in the beckside alders. Dipper and Grey Wagtail can be seen from the bridge over Grizedale Beck.

8 The feeding station at the cottage at the top of the lane is visited by Nuthatch and Marsh Tit. Look out for Red Squirrel at this locality.

9 Throughout the length of the north-bound route you have the opportunity to see all the previously mentioned woodland species – in essence, Redstart, Pied Flycatcher and Great Spotted Woodpecker in the deciduous areas and Goldcrest, Redpoll, Siskin and Crossbill in the coniferous.

10 The car-park on the east side of the road is visited by Jay and Nuthatch. Check the tops of the beech trees carefully for Hawfinch and Brambling, most regular in winter.

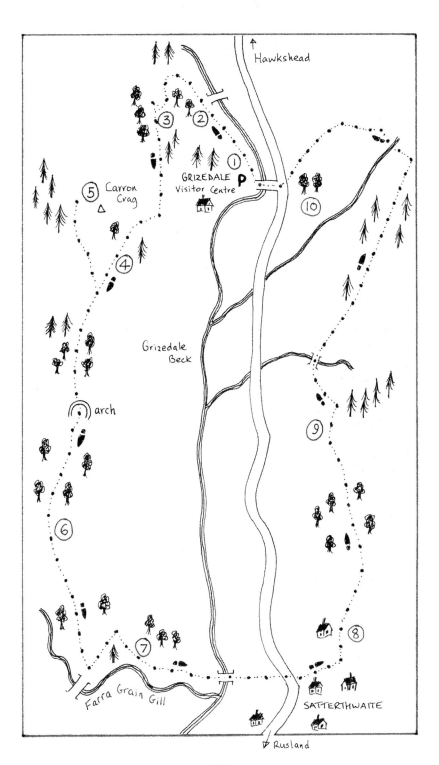

Hawkshead

GRIZEDALE
Visitor Centre

Carron
Crag

⑤

③ ②

①

⑩

④

Grizedale
Beck

arch

⑥

⑨

⑦

⑧

Farra Grain Gill

SATTERTHWAITE

Rusland

29

Torver & Coniston Water

Start: Torver   **Grid ref:** SD284942   **Distance:** 5½ miles/9 km
Maps: Landranger Sheet 96; Outdoor Leisure 6 *English Lakes (SW)*

A low-level walk which not only incorporates some of the Lake District's finest and most well-known scenery, but also provides a wide variety of bird species throughout the year. Choose a calm day so that wildfowl on Coniston Water are readily visible and not hidden by frustrating waves.

1 The patchwork area behind Torver can be very productive. The fields hold feeding Jackdaws and the hedgerows, especially in winter, are full of tits. Winter-time will also ensure flocks of finches and Yellowhammer, the garden at Crook being particularly good. Redwing and Fieldfare are in evidence in autumn and winter. Willow Warbler is numerous in spring and Buzzard haunts the woodland.

2 From the bridge over the A593, Dipper and Grey Wagtail can be seen.

3 The path down to the shores of Coniston Water provides a panoramic view over Torver Common Wood; Green Woodpecker and Great Spotted Woodpecker are resident here.

4 The small coniferous stand at the lake's edge harbours a wide variety of easily seen species in winter, with tit parties that include Long-tailed Tit, Marsh Tit, Treecreeper and Goldcrest.

5 Coniston Water is home to Mute Swan, Mallard, Tufted Duck, Pochard, Goldeneye, Goosander, Black-headed Gull and Cormorant. Roosting Cormorants can be seen on the guano-adorned trees of Fir Island on the east side. Rarer species such as Red-throated and Great Northern Diver, Red-necked Grebe, Scaup, Long-tailed Duck and Common Scoter have occurred in recent years.

6 The walk north will yield Mistle Thrush, Jay, Coal Tit, Green Woodpecker and Greenfinch. Look out for Siskin, in winter, among the lakeside alder trees. Siskin can also be regular in the grounds of Coniston Hall.

7 When the path turns sharply westwards, take advantage of the viewpoint to scan the reed areas. Little Grebe, Great Crested Grebe and Reed Bunting can be located, and Sedge Warbler breeds here.

8 The route along the old railway line produces common woodland species. Peregrine and Kestrel can be observed, the former's presence often given away by mobbing Jackdaws. Ravens can also be seen especially in winter when they descend from the heights of the Old Man of Coniston.

9 The gradual ascent along the contours of New Intake in summer often affords a glimpse of Cuckoo and the juniper and gorse bushes can hold Whinchat. The vantage point provides sightings of Woodcock roding over Bleanthwaite Coppice on warm evenings while Buzzard is regular at all times, as is Meadow Pipit.

10 The path crosses Torver Beck and descends on the south side. Dipper can be seen at this altitude, but it is much more common on the beck's lower stretches. Ring Ouzel may be seen here in spring.

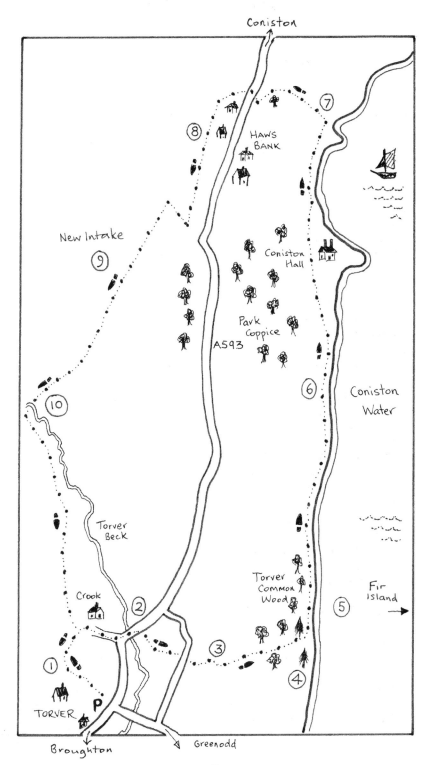

Coniston

⑦

HAWS
BANK

⑧

New Intake

⑨

Coniston
Hall

Park
Coppice

A593

⑥

Coniston
Water

⑩

Torver
Beck

Crook

②

Torver
Common
Wood

③

⑤

Fir
Island

④

①

TORVER

P

Broughton   Greenodd

31

The Levens & Rusland Valleys

Start: Backbarrow   **Grid ref:** SD355849   **Distance:** 7½ miles/12 km
Maps: Landranger Sheet 96; Outdoor Leisure 7 *English Lakes (SE)*

Although not totally essential, it is best to time this walk with a low tide when estuary birds can be seen feeding at the River Leven and Rusland Pool. There is plenty to see at all times of the year, but May can be tremendously productive with an abundance of summer visitors in all the different habitats.

1 From the bridge over the River Leven there are always Dipper and Grey Wagtail. Mute Swan, Goosander and Goldeneye can be seen in winter while in summer, the whole valley can be alive with Swallows, House Martins and Swifts.

2 The bridge over the railway provides an ideal viewing platform for woodland species such as Long-tailed Tit, Marsh Tit, Coal Tit, Willow Warbler and Redstart.

3 The uphill walk among deciduous woodland will yield trilling Wood Warbler, Blackcap, Garden Warbler, Willow Warbler and Goldcrest. Adders can be quite numerous! The summit affords excellent views over the whole valley. Buzzards will be in evidence, as will Redstart and Tree Pipit. Look out for the Green Hairstreak butterfly.

4 The descent takes you through Tree Pipit, Buzzard and Green Woodpecker country. The whole woodland on the south side is a Bluebell paradise. Abbots Reading Farm is another site for Redstart and also for Great Spotted Woodpecker.

5 The lane northwest past Abbots Reading has Goldfinch and Redstart and gives close range views of the substantial heronry in among the lone stand of Scots Pine. In the low-lying fields adjacent to Rusland Pool you should see Mallard, Shelduck and Snipe.

6 Hawfinch is regular in the woodland on the west side of Rusland Pool, Reed Bunting and Sedge Warbler should be encountered in wet hedgerows, and both Goosander and Common Sandpiper can be frequent.

7 On the Bouth circuit, Bullfinch haunt the woodland near Great Lindeth, and Spotted Flycatcher can be located in the village.

8 Buzzard is resident in all suitable woodland and as the estuary widens, Red-breasted Merganser should become commonplace. Look out for Meadow Pipit and Skylark in the open areas, and for Linnet, Reed Bunting and Whitethroat in the gorse clumps. In winter Greylag Geese and Whooper Swans utilise the fields.

9 The long riverine stretch northward will produce more Common Sandpipers and Red-breasted Mergansers, plus Siskin in winter, while Cuckoo can be obvious in Roudsea Wood Nature Reserve. Kingfisher, all too uncommon in Cumbria, breeds here.

10 The uphill path through Low Wood provides close proximity to all the woodland species.

11 Further views of Dipper and Grey Wagtail can be had from the narrow bridge over the River Leven.

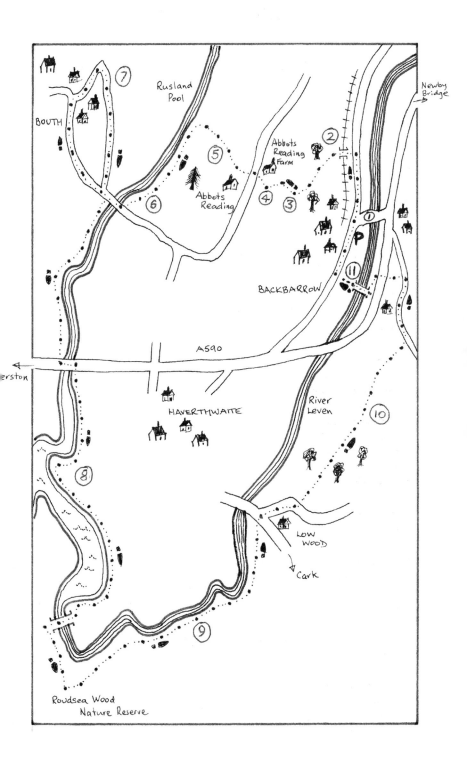

Flookburgh & Humphrey Head

Start: Flookburgh **Grid ref:** SD366756 **Distance:** 7 miles/11 km
Maps: Landranger Sheet 96; Outdoor Leisure 7 *English Lakes (SE)*

A further chance to familiarise yourself with the waders and wildfowl of Morecambe Bay. Aim to be at Humphrey Head at high tide in order to watch the mud flats being exposed. An 8.5 metre tide is probably the optimum.

1 Low-lying fields either side of the narrow lane to Humphrey Head are bordered by hedgerows which in spring can harbour migrants. In winter, Curlew and Lapwing are abundant, and both Woodpigeon and Stock Dove are frequent. Grey Heron can be found along damp field edges. Winter will also produce Meadow Pipit and Skylark, and Snipe can be flushed from the ditches. The lush vegetation around Holme can provide surprises. In some years a substantial flock of Tree Sparrows can be located.

2 The vegetated hollow is a haven for migrants especially in autumn when Goldcrests can be numerous. In winter, Coal Tit, Bullfinch, Redwing and Fieldfare utilise this location.

3 Humphrey Head Point overlooks the north side of Morecambe Bay. Great Crested Grebe, Red-breasted Merganser and Cormorant are all likely, and vast congregations of Oystercatcher and Dunlin can be seen roosting to the west on Out Marsh.

4 Humphrey Head Wood is home to Great Spotted Woodpecker, Green Woodpecker, Nuthatch, Blackcap and Chiffchaff. The receding tide will provide excellent views of Shelduck, Pintail, Oystercatcher, Ringed Plover, Grey Plover and various gulls, including Common.

5 The northward path to Allithwaite passes through typical Long-tailed Tit and Willow Warbler country. Scan the trees of Kirkhead Wood for Buzzard and Sparrowhawk.

6 The southward path passes a small wetland area which has Reed Bunting and Sedge Warbler, while the beck supports Dipper and Grey Wagtail. Watch out too for Goldfinch.

7 Redwing and Fieldfare will be found in winter in the woodland on the west of the uphill lane.

8 A superb view of Cartmel Priory and the southern Lake District can be had from the path that strikes west just north of Templand.

9 The woodland around Birkby Hall can be exceptionally productive. Goldcrest, Great Spotted Woodpecker, Bullfinch and Treecreeper can all be located, while in summer, Willow Warbler breeds here.

10 The southbound road provides an expansive view across the Cark Valley. Buzzard is regular and in the evenings Barn Owl can be seen hunting here. Large flocks of gulls and corvids feed in the low-lying fields.

11 The path south from Applebury Hill Farm is one of the few consistent Cumbrian sites for Red-legged Partridge.

12 The trees bordering the railway are wintering sites for Redwing and Fieldfare. Finch flocks, often with good numbers of Goldfinches, also use this site.

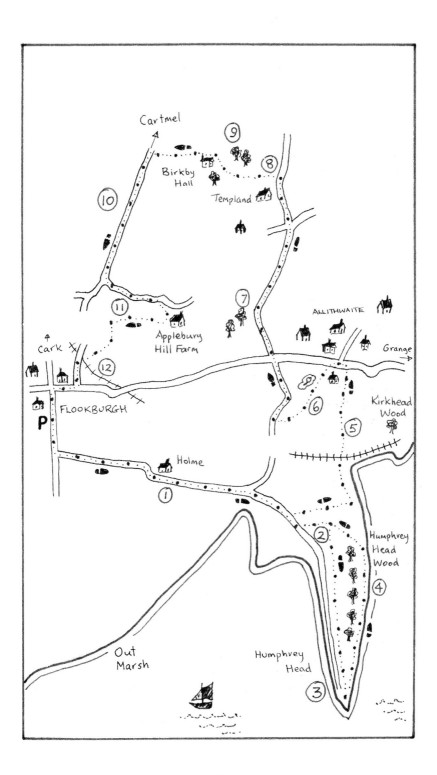

Grange & Hampsfield Fell

Start: Grange-over-Sands   **Grid ref:** SD412782   **Distance:** 6 miles/10 km
Maps: Landranger Sheet 97; Outdoor Leisure 7 *English Lakes (SE)*

There is a tremendous amount of variety concentrated in these six miles. The walk commences at Grange-over-Sands railway station from where the denizens of the Kent Estuary can be observed. The route takes in the deciduous woodland of Eggerslack, crosses the limestone pavement of Hampsfield Fell, descends into suburban Allithwaite and Grange before the wide expanse of mudflats is encountered again. A mid to low tide provides the best birdwatching.

1 The mudflats of the Kent Estuary are feeding grounds for Mallard, Shelduck, Pintail, Redshank, Oystercatcher, Curlew and scores of gulls. Grey Phalarope and Pectoral Sandpiper have both been recorded from this area in recent years. Great Crested Grebe, Cormorant and Red-breasted Merganser can be viewed further out in mid-channel, accompanied by winter Goldeneye.

2 There is the opportunity for studying duck and goose identification at Grange wildfowl pond – bring a loaf of bread and your camera. The gardens are also home to Collared Dove and can support finch flocks in winter – Brambling, Siskin and Redpoll have all been here in recent years.

3 All the typical Cumbrian woodland bird species can be found in Eggerslack Wood. Patience can be rewarded by sightings of Tawny Owl, Jay, Nuthatch and Great Spotted Woodpecker. In winter, the trees can be alive with Redwing and Fieldfare, many of them roosting in the yew trees.

4 Upon leaving the wood, the uphill walk across limestone pavement provides wonderful all-round views, culminating in the panorama from atop the Hospice. Being above the wood provides the opportunity to glimpse the bounding flight of Green Woodpecker. Meadow Pipit, Skylark and Yellowhammer can all be met with, the last-named utilising the scrub hawthorn.

5 The walk into Allithwaite passes the Golf Course and Cemetery, both venues having had Waxwing in previous winters. Low-lying fields are home to gull flocks in winter while the woodland around Jack Hill supports Sparrowhawk, Kestrel, Greenfinch and Goldfinch.

6 At Kents Bank railway station a small pool to the south holds Moorhen, Coot, Sedge Warbler and Reed Bunting. In winter-time, this is probably the best viewing point for Pintail, their closeness depends upon the state of the tide. Mallard and Shelduck are also easily viewable as are Redshank and Oystercatcher. The wide open expanses are hunting grounds for Merlin and Peregrine.

7 An incoming or receding tide will see an enormous amount of activity around the Kent Channel. Depending upon the time of year, you are likely to see Knot and Dunlin, possibly Bar-tailed Godwit, Goosander and Red-breasted Merganser and an abundance of gulls, probably at least five species. It is well worth scrutinising the gulls: Yellow-legged Gull and Mediterranean Gull have occurred on the Kent Estuary.

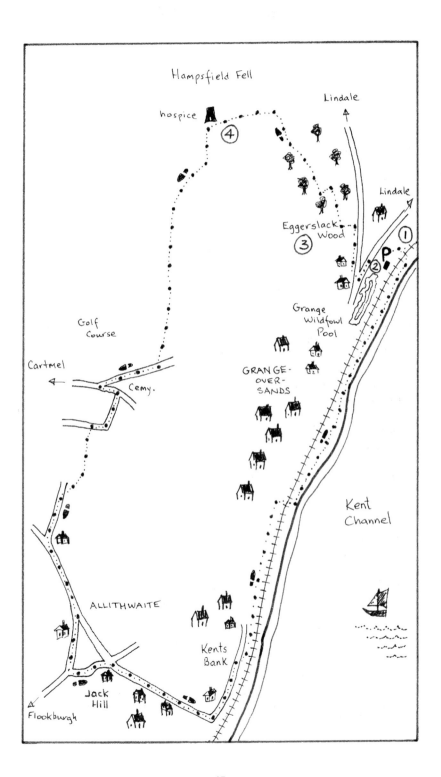

Hampsfield Fell

hospice

④

Lindale

Lindale

Eggerslack
Wood

③

P

①

②

Grange
Wildfowl
Pool

Golf
Course

Cartmel

Cemy.

GRANGE-
OVER-
SANDS

Kent
Channel

ALLITHWAITE

Kents
Bank

Jack
Hill

Flookburgh

Foulshaw & Whitbarrow

Start: A590 Sampool **Grid ref:** SD469853 **Distance:** 9 miles/14 km
Maps: Landranger Sheet 97; Outdoor Leisure 7 *English Lakes (SE)*

This is a longish walk, full of variety, which encompasses a range of habitats from sea-level along the River Kent and Milnthorpe Sands to an altitude of 75 metres on the south side of Whitbarrow Scar. In order to maximise your birdwatching, a mid to low tide is preferential to view the feeding and roosting birds.

1 The meandering River Gilpin is at times adjacent to the track and provides sightings of wildfowl which in summer will include Mute Swan, Mallard and Shelduck. Winter will probably be more productive and should include Wigeon, Teal, Goldeneye, Goosander and Red-breasted Merganser. Smew has been noted from this site and Cormorant and Lapwing are usually in evidence.

2 At High Foulshaw, the path follows the embankment and affords excellent views of the mud flats. A wide range of gulls will be on view, flanked by Cormorant and sentinel Grey Heron. Waders are strongly represented by Redshank, Oystercatcher and Lapwing, but sightings of rarer birds have included Green Sandpiper, Avocet and Black-winged Pratincole. The hedgerows support Chaffinch flocks in winter and Reed Bunting can be seen at all times of the year.

3 The saltmarsh in winter often harbours shelter-seeking Meadow Pipit, Skylark, Reed Bunting and Chaffinch, while in spring and autumn, it is a feeding ground for Pied Wagtail. The mudflats can teem with Curlew and Shelduck.

4 Picnic at Birkswood Point. An incoming tide will push Shelduck, Redshank, Oystercatcher and Curlew towards you, while out in the channel, Red-breasted Merganser sail past.

5 From the bridge over the Main Drain, Moorhen and Reed Bunting can be seen, and in spring-time Sedge Warbler can be heard.

6 Above the woodland of Ulpha Fell, Buzzard can be watched at all times of the year. However, a warm March afternoon will see peak pre-breeding season activity; listen for them mewing. Kestrel and Great Spotted Woodpecker can be located at any time during this walk, and in spring-time there are usually concentrations of gulls and Lapwing in the fields just south of the A590.

7 The delightful circuitous route through Town End can produce a whole host of surprises. Summer-time can yield Chiffchaff, Blackcap, Whitethroat, Willow and Garden Warbler, while winter provides Siskin, Redpoll, Bullfinch and Goldcrest.

8 Grey Wagtail is regular at magical Beck Head, and the berry-bearing trees are havens for winter Fieldfare and Redwing.

9 The contour walk along the edge of White Scar affords panoramic views of Foulshaw. Limestone fossils litter the edge of the path and in summer the air is alive with bird song. Excellent birdwatching near Raven's Lodge should include Peregrine, Kestrel and Raven.

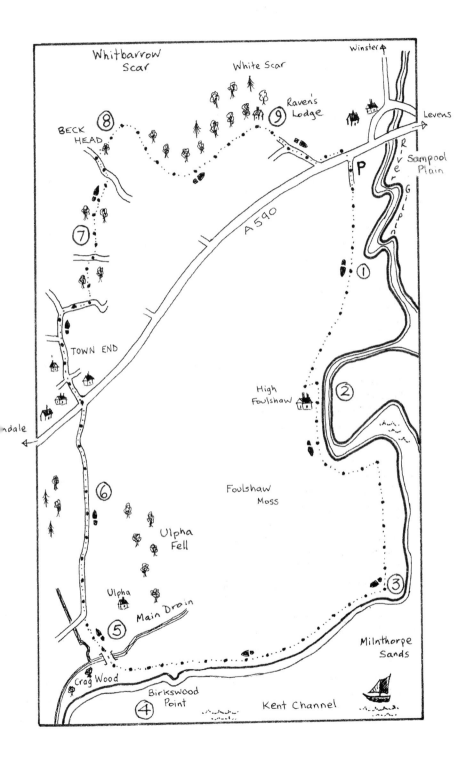

Milnthorpe & Storth Woods

Start: Milnthorpe   **Grid ref:** SD498815   **Distance:** 6 miles/10 km
Maps: Landranger Sheet 97; Outdoor Leisure 7 *English Lakes (SE)*

This walk is best done to coincide with either low tide or a moderate rising or falling tide. Extreme spring tides, albeit visually spectacular in themselves, force the birds to totally vacate the Kent Channel and Milnthorpe Sands. 10 metre tides have been known to inundate the road at Sandside and even witnessed a windsurfer astride his board on the B5282!

1 The riverside walk along the River Bela from Milnthorpe can be extremely productive at all times of the year. In winter, foraging parties of Long-tailed Tit may be accompanied by Goldcrest and Treecreeper, while near the footbridge and road bridge the water holds Mallard, Tufted Duck, Pochard, Goldeneye, Red-breasted Merganser and elusive Little Grebe. Kingfisher is not unknown here. Swallow, Sand Martin and House Martin feed here during summer.

2 The parkland of Dallam Towers is home to a magnificent herd of Fallow Deer. Pheasant, Mistle Thrush and Green Woodpecker are present at all times and Tree Pipit can be seen displaying in summer. There can be up to 60 Grey Heron nests at Dallam Towers, and they can be observed easily from the park. The mature trees hold Sparrowhawk, Great Spotted Woodpecker and Hawfinch.

3 A small, un-named tarn to the east of Haverbrack holds Mallard, Teal, Coot, Moorhen and Long-tailed Tit in the winter and the lanes and paths to Storth in spring-time fall under the spell of singing summer migrants such as Willow Warbler, Blackcap and Garden Warbler.

4 The mud flats of the Kent Channel are feeding grounds for Shelduck, Oystercatcher, Redshank, Curlew, Black-headed Gull and roosting sites for Common, Herring, Great Black-backed and Lesser Black-backed Gull, Cormorant and Grey Heron. The waters of the Kent Channel yield Red-breasted Merganser, Goosander and in winter, Goldeneye.

5 The route takes in limestone woodland to the south of Storth and continues with a brief detour to Hazelslack Tower before heading east to the Fairy Steps – breathe in deeply as you feed yourself between the rocks. At all times of the year you are likely to encounter Collared Dove near habitation and Bullfinch, Nuthatch and Hawfinch in the well-wooded areas. Hawfinch is notoriously difficult to see anywhere due mainly to its shyness. The species has a tendency to sit at the top of a tree or close to the top, so any bird atop a tree is well worth scrutinising. Persevere with every bird, and eventually you will be rewarded with a sighting of Britain's largest and most spectacular finch. Underlaid Wood during the winter can be home to hundreds of roosting Redwing and Fieldfare.

6 The vegetation of Whin Scar holds breeding Goldcrest and Coal Tit.

7 Mallard, Dipper and Grey Wagtail can be seen on the River Bela at Beetham.

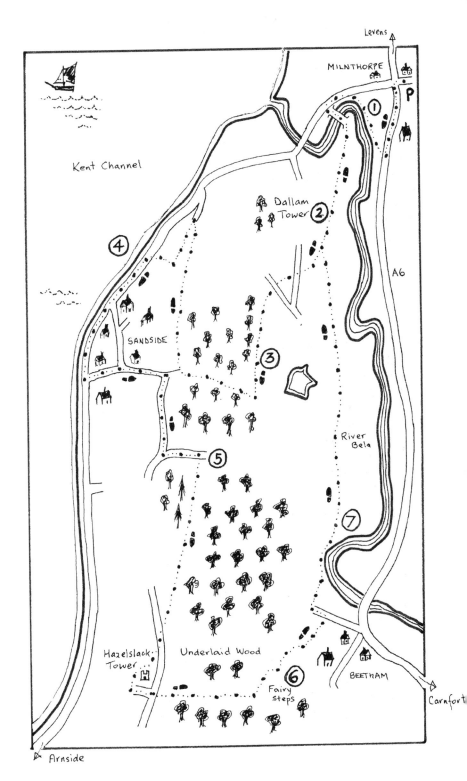

Levens

MILNTHORPE

P

①

Kent Channel

Dallam
Tower ②

④

A6

SANDSIDE

③

River
Bela

⑤

⑦

Hazelslack
Tower

Underlaid Wood

⑥

BEETHAM

Fairy
steps

Carnforth

Arnside

Arnside & Silverdale

Start: Arnside   **Grid ref:** SD454786   **Distance:** 6 miles/10 km
Maps: Landranger Sheet 97; Outdoor Leisure 7 *English Lakes (SE)*

The Arnside and Silverdale peninsula is carved out of limestone and heavily clothed in woodland. The combination of sylvan and estuarine habitat yields a walk which provides a wide variety of birds. It's a walk for any time of the year and not overly dependent upon a high tide; indeed too high a tide can result in a dearth of birds – their usual roosting sites being underwater.

1 The car-park on the promenade provides one of the most convenient birdwatching sites in the county. Shelduck, Redshank and Oystercatcher feed on the mud, while in the channels Grey Heron, Mallard, Red-breasted Merganser and Goosander can be seen. The area is a safe roost site for Cormorant and six species of gull, including Yellow-legged Gull, this being a regular location for this species.

2 Typical woodland birds such as Greenfinch, Chaffinch, Song Thrush and Mistle Thrush, Robin, Dunnock, Wren, Chiffchaff and Nuthatch can be found at Beach Wood.

3 Grubbins Wood has all the above species plus Great Spotted Woodpecker and Jay.

4 The saltmarsh channels at New Barns usually support a good number of Redshank, while Pied Wagtail, Meadow Pipit and Skylark can often be found on the short turf especially in autumn and winter.

5 Frith Wood holds all the usual woodland birds and is a regular site for Blackcap and Green Woodpecker.

6 A slight scramble from the beach up to a ledge provides a wonderful relaxed view of the channel and sands across to Holme Island and Grange-over-Sands. Winter-time birds will include Great Crested Grebe and Goldeneye, but almost anything may be glimpsed such as storm-driven Razorbill or Guillemot. Even a pod of Pilot Whales has been seen from here.

7 After negotiating the woodland of Arnside Park, where every caravan dweller seems to feed the birds, another estuary vista unfolds at Far Arnside and in winter can usually produce feeding flocks of Knot, Dunlin, Redshank and Oystercatcher. Bullfinch is regular at the caravan site entrance.

8 The open parkland of Middlebarrow Plain provides the opportunity to see Mistle Thrush and Green Woodpecker at all times, and Tree Pipit in the summer.

9 The saltmarsh at Red Rake is home at high tide in winter to Redshank, Oystercatcher and Wigeon.

10 The hedgerows of the lane to Arnside Tower can hold in winter Reed Bunting, Yellowhammer, a variety of finches, Redwing and Fieldfare. In summer look out for Redstart and Spotted Flycatcher. The low fields are home to Pheasant, Curlew, and Wheatear and Whinchat in spring and autumn. West of the tower can be seen Mallard, Teal, Grey Heron, Coot and Moorhen.

11 Arnside Knott Wood supports Treecreeper, Goldcrest, Great Spotted Woodpecker, Marsh Tit and in winter Redwing, Fieldfare, Siskin and Redpoll.

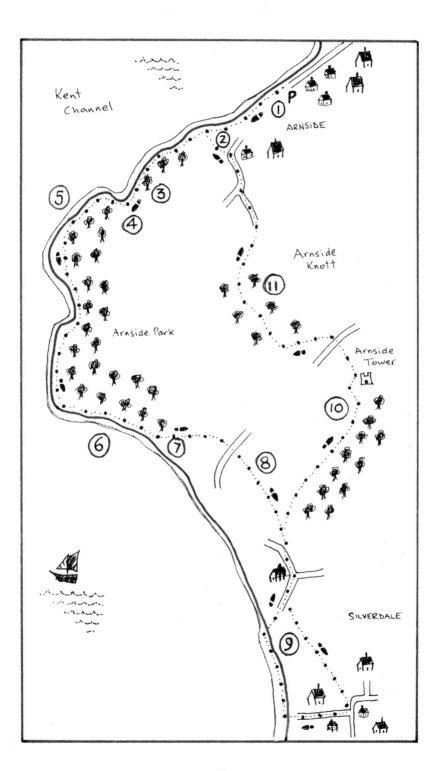

Kent Channel

ARNSIDE

Arnside Knott

Arnside Park

Arnside Tower

SILVERDALE

WALK 20

Natland & Levens Park

Start: Natland   **Grid ref:** SD 521893   **Distance:** 6 miles/10 km
Maps: Landranger Sheet 97; Outdoor Leisure 7 *English Lakes (SE)*

This very linear walk follows two waterways – one with water, the River Kent, and the other without, the disused Kendal to Lancaster canal. It's a walk for any time of the year, but bird-wise is undoubtedly best in spring and early summer when the first summer migrants have taken up residence. It is essential to keep to the designated paths in Levens Park.

1 The focus of Natland village is the green and church. Jackdaw, Collared Dove, Greenfinch and Goldfinch are normally present at all times; in summer, House Martin, Swallow and Swift hawk for insects. Look out for Goldcrest in the evergreens during winter.

2 The open fields in the vicinity of Larkrigg support assemblies of gulls, chiefly Black-headed and Common, and Lapwing in the winter.

3 The woodland at Larkrigg Spring in spring-time can be alive with the songs of Willow Warbler and Blackcap. Spotted Flycatcher breeds here. Sparrowhawk, Tree-creeper, Great Spotted Woodpecker and a variety of tits, including Long-tailed, make the wood their home throughout the year.

4 The walk through Sedgwick can normally produce Goldfinch, and in summer plenty of Swallow and House Martin.

5 The River Kent in Levens Park can be exceptionally productive, especially if, at various locations, the birdwatcher stops walking and waits and watches. Patience can often be rewarded by a glimpse of a Kingfisher, sometimes no more than a flash of brilliant blue. You may discover the Kingfisher perched if you scrutinise branches overhanging the quieter parts of the river. Dipper, Grey Wagtail and Goosander may be seen anywhere along the river's course, but Mute Swan and Grey Heron are usually found at the southernmost end, as is Common Sandpiper in summer.

6 The tree-lined avenue in Levens Park is populated by Pheasant and a flock of Bagot goats. It is also home to one of Cumbria's rarest breeding woodland birds, the Lesser Spotted Woodpecker. A survey in 1996 indicated that there were probably no more than seven pairs in the county. You should see Nuthatch and Great Spotted Woodpecker throughout the year, and Redstart, Spotted and Pied Flycatcher in the spring and summer.

7 On calm summer evenings, bats can be seen feeding in numbers just to the east of the bridge. Sand Martin, House Martin and Swallow can be seen doing the same, and Dipper often disappears through the bridge.

8 The forces on the River Kent to the north of the dual carriageway are localities all year for Dipper, Grey Wagtail and Goosander. In the quieter areas, Grey Heron is often met with as is Mallard.

9 An encounter with a Kingfisher can occur at any time; Siskin and Redpoll may be seen in winter. Red Squirrel has been noted on many occasions in Low Park Wood.

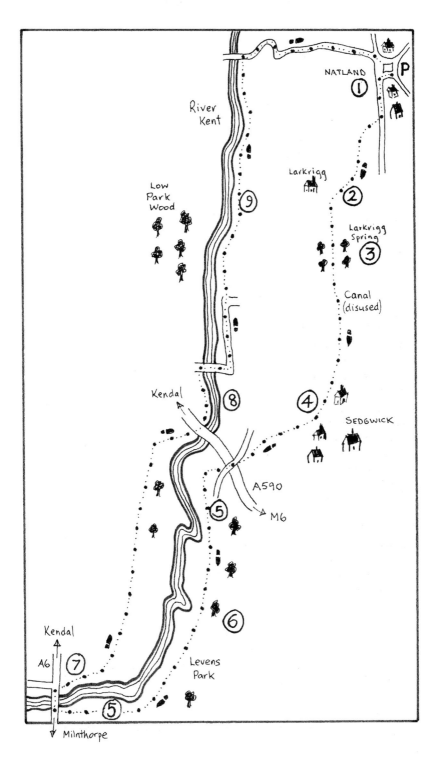

River
Kent

NATLAND
①

P

Larkrigg
②

Low
Park
Wood

⑨

Larkrigg
Spring
③

Canal
(disused)

Kendal

⑧

④

SEDGWICK

A590

⑤

→ M6

⑥

Levens
Park

Kendal

A6   ⑦

⑤

↓ Milnthorpe

Burneside & Staveley

Start: Burneside **Grid ref:** SD505957 **Distance:** 6½ miles/10.5 km
Maps: Landranger Sheet 97; Outdoor Leisure 7 *English Lakes (SE)*

This walk commences at Burneside and follows the River Kent upstream past Bowston
and Cowen Head to Staveley. From here an easterly detour to higher elevations ensues
before picking up the River Kent again. Bird-wise it can be an incredibly productive
walk with a mixture of woodland and water birds, and is undoubtedly one of the best
Dipper stretches in south Cumbria.

1 The churchyard at Burneside is a regular haunt for Collared Dove, Bullfinch and
in winter, Goldcrest.

2 From the paper mill bridge watch for Little Grebe, Goosander, Mallard, Grey
Wagtail and Long-tailed Tit. Small flocks of Siskin and Redpoll have been noted
from the trees around the small housing estate.

3 The screening plantation provides sheltered habitat for Willow Warbler in summer
and mixed tit parties, plus Goldcrest and Treecreeper at other times. Occasionally
the area holds a winter finch roost which has included Brambling in past years.

4 The open fields in some winters can support large flocks of Woodpigeon and Stock
Dove. Redwing and Fieldfare can be seen foraging in frost-free times.

5 In the calmer waters of the River Kent are found Mallard, Tufted Duck, Little
Grebe, Cormorant, Coot, and Goosander. On windless summer days Sand Martin,
House Martin and Swallow will be seen hawking for insects. Kingfisher breed on
the River Kent and patient observation of overhanging branches above some of the
quieter stretches of water may be rewarded. Dipper can be found at all times of
the year along the length of this walk and in spring-time listen out for its delightful
quirky song. The riverside trees can provide sightings of Redpoll, Siskin, Long-tailed
Tit and Goldfinch. Small numbers of Grey Heron may be spotted in the fields on
the west side of the river.

6 The gorge-like section of the river provides almost face-to-face encounters with
Dipper, and Grey Wagtail can often be seen searching for insects along the riverside
rocks. Black-headed and Common Gull frequent the sewage works.

7 Mallard, Goosander and Dipper utilise the River Kent in Staveley and once across
the bridge, look out for Bullfinch and Coal Tit.

8 The uphill walk alongside Craggy Plantation provides commanding views across the
valley towards Kendal and beyond. Buzzard should be fairly evident especially during
spring-time courtship display. Listen for their mewing call.

9 The garden at Frost Hole is a winter haven for a variety of tits and finches, plus
Goldcrest and Yellowhammer. The downhill walk past the mine adits should yield
Siskin and Redpoll, while Crossbill has been recorded from the conifer wood to the
west of the track.

10 The Woodland Trust wood is delightful in spring with the songs of Willow Warbler,
Chiffchaff and Blackcap.

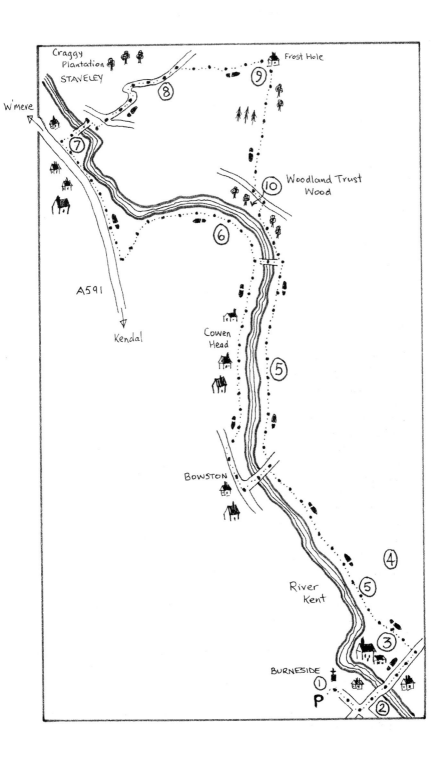

Craggy
Plantation
STAVELEY

Frost Hole

⑨

⑧

W'mere

⑦

A591

Kendal

Woodland Trust
Wood

⑩

⑥

Cowen
Head

⑤

Bowston

④

River
Kent

⑤

③

BURNESIDE

①

P

②

White Moss Common & Elterwater

Start: White Moss Common **Grid ref:** NY348066 **Distance:** 5½ miles/9 km
Maps: Landranger Sheet 90; Outdoor Leisure 7 *English Lakes (SE)*

This wonderful circuit takes in some of the Lake District's finest views as it meanders from the western end of Rydal Water to Elter Water and Loughrigg Tarn. There is an excellent mix of birds provided by woodland, open water and river. The woodland can be exquisite in spring and summer, while the open water comes to the fore in winter, providing a refuge for winter wildfowl.

1 Pochard, Goldeneye, Tufted Duck and Goosander are resident on Rydal Water in winter.

2 The woodland of Baneriggs in summer holds Willow Warbler, Pied Flycatcher, Redstart and Chiffchaff. Throughout the year Nuthatch, Great Spotted Woodpecker and a variety of tits are present, while in winter Redpoll, Siskin, Treecreeper and Goldcrest can all be located. Look out for winter finch flocks – the most abundant will be Chaffinch, but often accompanying them are Brambling.

3 At the southern end of Grasmere, Grey Wagtail and Dipper can be seen all year and Common Sandpiper may be met with in spring. The open water is home to Tufted Duck, Pochard, Goldeneye, Goosander, Red-breasted Merganser, Mallard, Coot, Little Grebe, Cormorant, Mute Swan, Greylag and Canada Goose. Rarer ducks such as Scaup and Long-tailed Duck sometimes occur.

4 The lane to the east of Hunting Stile is an excellent locality for Nuthatch, Great Spotted Woodpecker, Jay and Red Squirrel. A bird table at the northern end of the lane is favoured by all four, and has had flocks of Brambling and Chaffinch in winter. In summer the woodland is alive with songs of Willow Warbler, Blackcap and Redstart.

5 The open country of Huntingstile Crag should afford encounters with Meadow Pipit and Skylark, Cuckoo in summer, aerial battles between Buzzard and Raven, and magnificent views especially to the west.

6 The route follows Great Langdale Beck from Elterwater to Skelwith Bridge. Along the river are found Dipper, Grey Wagtail, Pied Wagtail and even Kingfisher. In the riverside trees are Siskin, Redpoll and Long-tailed Tit.

7 Elter Water is home in winter to Pochard, Tufted Duck, Goldeneye, Goosander, Red-breasted Merganser and occasionally Whooper Swan. Throughout the year the site holds Great Crested Grebe, Little Grebe, Mallard, Mute Swan, Coot and Moorhen.

8 The oak woodland of Neaum Wood is one of Cumbria's Nuthatch strongholds, the species flourishing with the help of a plethora of bird tables. Birdwatching can be exceptionally good here with close range views of Great Spotted Woodpecker and Red Squirrel at bird tables a near-certainty. Sparrowhawk also uses the bird table as a feeding station!

9 Like other areas of open water on this walk, Loughrigg Tarn is favoured by winter diving duck, including Goosander, and an abundance of Coot and Moorhen.

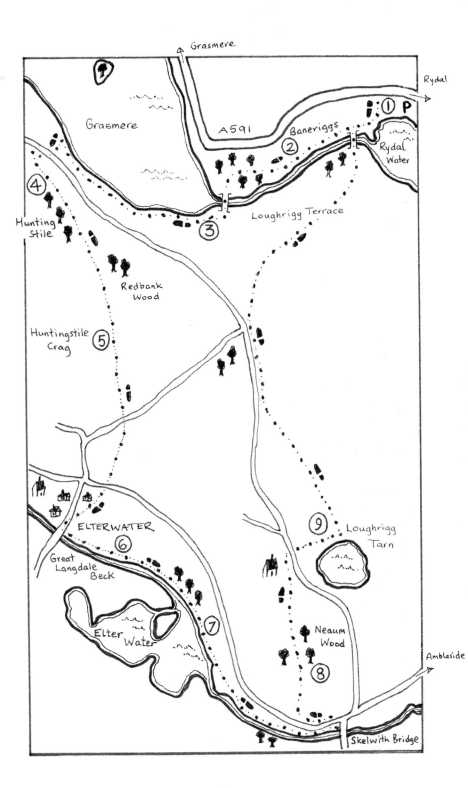

Grasmere

Rydal

Grasmere

A591

Baneriggs

① P

②

Rydal Water

③

Loughrigg Terrace

④

Hunting Stile

Redbank Wood

Huntingstile Crag

⑤

ELTERWATER

⑥

Great Langdale Beck

Elter Water

⑦

⑨

Loughrigg Tarn

Neaum Wood

⑧

Ambleside

Skelwith Bridge

49

Kirkby Lonsdale & Barbon

Start: Kirkby Lonsdale **Grid ref:** SD615783 **Distance:** 7 miles/11 km
Maps: Landranger Sheet 97; Outdoor Leisure 2 *Yorkshire Dales (South & West)*

River valleys such as the Lune are migration avenues utilised throughout the bird-year but are of particular importance in spring and autumn. This walk incorporates not only this spectacular river but also the lower reaches of Barbon Beck tumbling down from Middleton Fell, and woodland and bridleways set in the shadow of the fells.

1 Devil's Bridge on the eastern side of Kirkby Lonsdale provides a superb vantage point and the longer you linger, the more you will see. Winter viewing should provide Mallard, Goosander, Dipper and Grey Wagtail and the riverside trees can be host to parties of tits, Siskin and Redpoll. In summer Swallow, House Martin, Sand Martin and Swift can often be seen hawking over the waters.

2 The open parkland surrounding Casterton Hall can, with patience, produce Green and Great Spotted Woodpecker, Mistle Thrush, Nuthatch, Greenfinch and Goldfinch at all times. During the summer months, the area is home to Cuckoo and Tree Pipit, the latter with its wonderful display flight, singing and parachuting at the same time.

3 The woodland to the north of the hall can be alive with warblers such as Blackcap, Garden, Willow and Chiffchaff in spring and summer. Additionally, it may be possible to find both Spotted Flycatcher and Redstart. Winter will yield small parties of Siskin and Redpoll and throughout the year Long-tailed Tit, Marsh Tit, Tree-creeper and Goldcrest are present. Bullfinch, often first detected by their rather melancholy soft whistle, breed here. They can be shy birds and often all you may see is a vanishing white rump.

4 The northward path alongside Barbon Beck is very productive. Not only should you see Dipper, Grey Wagtail, Pied Wagtail and Reed Bunting, but also Grey Heron, Mallard, Teal and Snipe. In spring-time listen out for the rattling song or harsh scolding of Whitethroat.

5 The overview of the valley and woodland of Barbondale is well worth a prolonged stay. Displaying Buzzard and Sparrowhawk over the wood are a feature especially of calm spring days. They are not early risers and prefer to wait for the air to warm before using these updraughts to aid their display. Kestrel and Cuckoo are also regularly sighted in this area and east of the road, along the fell margin, Skylark, Meadow Pipit, Wheatear, Linnet and Yellowhammer can all be seen.

6 Tuplot Wood is home to Willow Warbler, Chiffchaff, Blackcap, and Spotted Flycatcher in summer, while Sparrowhawk, Great Spotted Woodpecker and Tree-creeper should all be present the whole year.

7 Meadow Pipit, Skylark, Wheatear, Whinchat, Linnet and Yellowhammer are likely to be encountered along Fellfoot Road. The abundance of small birds and the open country makes it an ideal hunting ground for migrating Merlin.

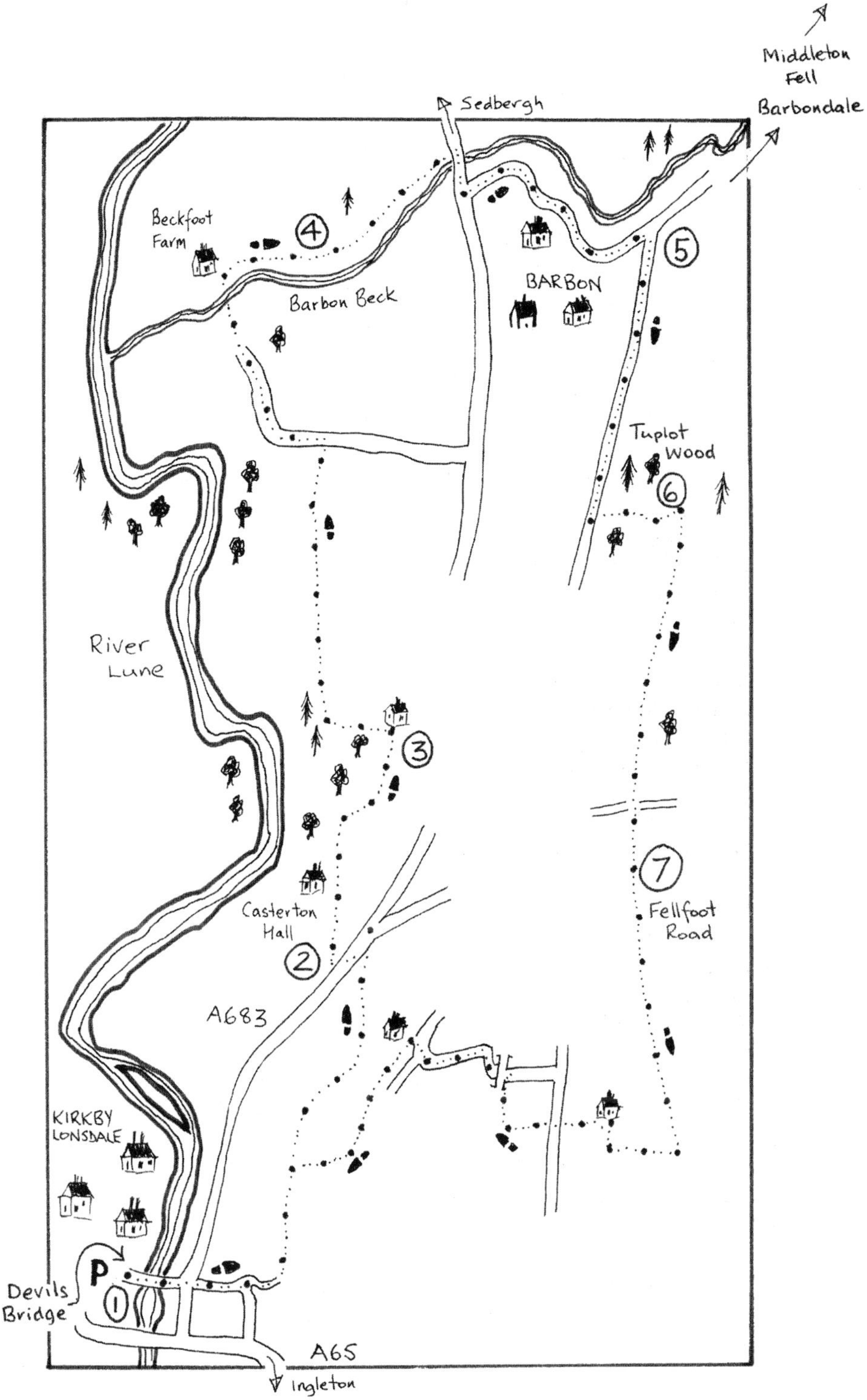

Middleton
Fell
Barbondale

Sedbergh

Beckfoot
Farm

④

Barbon Beck

⑤

BARBON

Tuplot
Wood

⑥

River
Lune

③

Casterton
Hall

②

A683

⑦

Fellfoot
Road

KIRKBY
LONSDALE

P

Devils
Bridge

①

A65

Ingleton

51

Killington & River Lune

Start: Old Scotch Road   **Grid ref:** SD599911   **Distance:** 7 miles/11 km

Maps: Landranger Sheet 97; Outdoor Leisure Sheets 2, 7 & 19

This walk in the southeast of the county takes in two of Cumbria's lesser known waters, Killington Reservoir and Lily Mere, and follows the River Lune north for a mile. Consequently, there are water birds aplenty, plus the chance to see some moorland specialities in New Park.

1 Walk west along the reservoir's southern road as far as the dam. Killington is a major haunt for a number of birds and a telescope increases the enjoyment. Breeding birds include Great Crested Grebe, Tufted Duck, Red-breasted Merganser, Canada Goose, Moorhen, Coot, Oystercatcher, Lapwing, Redshank, Common Sandpiper, Black-headed Gull and Rook. Small numbers of Pochard, Goldeneye, Wigeon and Teal occur in winter along with Cormorant, Mallard and a substantial roost of Common and Black-headed Gulls. Little Gull and Black Tern are annual, usually in May. The site has recorded such exotics as Caspian Tern, Crane, Golden Oriole, Hobby and Ring-necked Duck.

2 Old Park's extensive woodland holds a typical array of species including Buzzard, Sparrowhawk, Green Woodpecker, Great Spotted Woodpecker, Treecreeper, Goldcrest and Jay throughout the year, with a summer supplement of Chiffchaff, Blackcap, Willow and Garden Warbler, and Fieldfare, Redwing, Siskin and Redpoll in winter.

3 The track to Aikrigg should provide Meadow Pipit, Skylark, Pied Wagtail, Swallow and Cuckoo in summer.

4 The hamlet of Killington, with the delightful Killington Hall, is just a nice place to be.

5 The northward walk along the River Lune provides the usual riverside fare of Grey Heron, Mallard, Goosander, Dipper and Grey Wagtail. Kingfisher is elusive but does occur here, and in winter Goldeneye is sometimes frequent, while in summer Common Sandpiper is met with. The riverside trees, most often birch and alder, support winter parties of tits which include Marsh and Long-tailed, with Siskin and Redpoll.

6 The route via Grassrigg and Greenholme on to the moorland of New Park takes you through Buzzard and Sparrowhawk country. The increase in altitude provides a good vantage point for scanning across the River Lune. New Park can be excellent, but at times, especially in winter, may appear barren. The area is the spring, summer and autumn haunt of Meadow Pipit, Skylark, Wheatear and Yellowhammer, and Kestrel hunts the rough ground. Short-eared Owl and Hen Harrier are both noted from this area, and the former is regular and most frequently seen in the morning or at dusk.

7 Lily Mere is one of the least watched sites in the county. It looks an ideal site to see migrating Osprey. In winter, the water holds Goldeneye, Pochard, small numbers of Teal and Wigeon and a roost of Common and Black-headed Gull. Mallard, Tufted Duck, Coot and Moorhen occur all year.

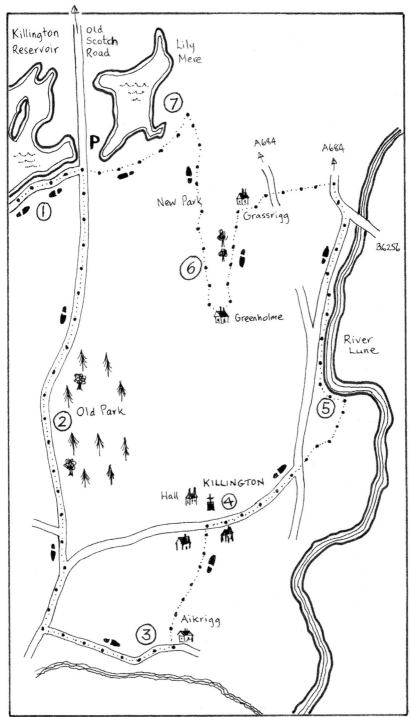

A684

Killington
Reservoir

old
Scotch
Road

Lily
Mere

P

⑦

A684

A684

New Park

Grassrigg

B6256

⑥

①

Greenholme

River
Lune

⑤

Old Park

②

KILLINGTON

Hall ⛪ ④

③ Aikrigg

Claife Heights

Start: Near Ferry House   **Grid ref:** SD388954   **Distance:** 6 miles/9.5 km
Maps: Landranger Sheet 97; Outdoor Leisure 7 *English Lakes (SE)*

Claife Heights on the western side of Windermere is for the most part clothed in conifer trees, not everybody's favourite. However there are a few bird species which favour this habitat and the woodland is home to both Crossbill and Long-eared Owl, two elusive Cumbrian species.

1 This particular narrow stretch of Lake Windermere is one of the best birdwatching areas on the lake. In summer there are Red-breasted Merganser, Tufted Duck, Mallard and Common Sandpiper, while winter yields Great Crested Grebe, Cormorant, Pochard, Goldeneye and a Black-headed Gull roost. Sightings of rarer species also occur quite regularly and have included Red-throated, Black-throated and Great Northern Diver, Red-necked Grebe, Common Scoter and Long-tailed Duck.

2 The path strikes northwest through Station Scar Wood. This superb little woodland has all the usual species of tit (including Marsh), Chiffchaff, Blackcap, Garden, Wood and Willow Warbler, Nuthatch, Redstart, Pied Flycatcher, Hawfinch and Woodcock.

3 The country opens out to the west at Mitchell Knotts. Consequently, summer-time will see displaying Tree Pipit and this is a good location for Cuckoo. Throughout the year Green Woodpecker, Meadow Pipit, Skylark and Yellowhammer should be evident. In the winter, large numbers of Woodpigeon and smaller numbers of Stock Dove roost in the surrounding trees, and there are always sightings of Raven which no doubt nest in the vicinity. Listen out for its far-carrying *'kronk, kronk'* call.

4 The extensive conifer areas can be unrewarding but this habitat harbours some real gems. Stealth and patience are the keys for seeing species in conifer woodland. This particular area holds Sparrowhawk, Long-eared Owl, Goldcrest, Long-tailed Tit, Coal Tit, Redpoll and Siskin. Possibly one of the most productive areas is at Three Dubs Tarn where all the above species have been seen.

5 At Hollin Band Plantation crossroads, the path heads southwest. This particular locality, with its mixture of deciduous and coniferous forest, has been a breeding site for Crossbill. Both Siskin and Redpoll can occur here in sizeable flocks especially during hard winters.

6 Wise Een Tarn and Moss Eccles Tarn support Tufted Duck, Pochard, Goldeneye and Mallard in the winter, and around their soft margins can be found Snipe and occasionally, Jack Snipe. A close relative, the Woodcock, can be seen 'roding' on calm summer evenings. Listen out for its strange gurgling calls.

7 Roe Deer are frequently seen crossing from the woodland of Cuckoo Brow Wood into that of Oatmeal Crag. Likewise, birds such as Green Woodpecker and Great Spotted Woodpecker can be seen flying across the gap. Buzzard and Sparrowhawk utilise the warm updraughts for display purposes.

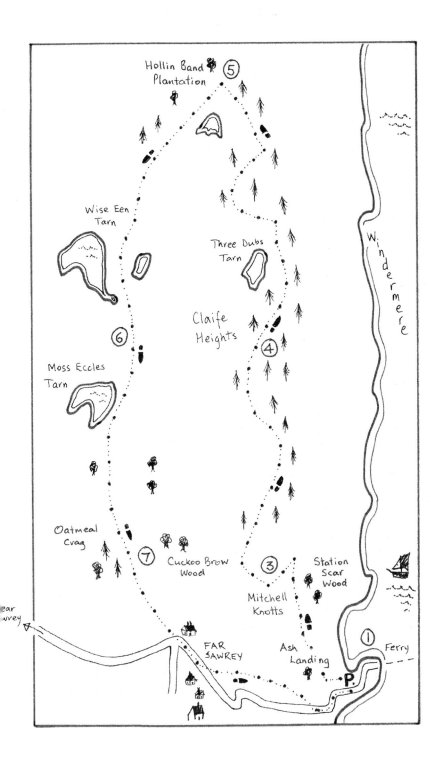

Hollin Band Plantation ⑤

Wise Een Tarn

Three Dubs Tarn

Claife Heights

⑥

Moss Eccles Tarn

④

Oatmeal Crag

⑦

Cuckoo Brow Wood

③

Station Scar Wood

Mitchell Knotts

Windermere

ar wrey

FAR SAWREY

Ash Landing

P

① Ferry

The High Street Horseshoe

Start: head of Haweswater **Grid ref:** NY469107 **Distance:** 7 miles/11 km

Maps: Landranger Sheet 90; Outdoor Leisure 5 & 7: *English Lakes (NE & SE)*

A fine walk in spectacular country. Proper mountain clothes and boots are pre-requisites. The path is rough, and the route difficult to follow when clouds are down; it may be best to avoid the walk then, unless you are experienced at route-finding by compass or GPS.

1 Up to Nan Bield Pass, skirting the north side of Harter Fell; listen for the song of Ring Ouzel. Small Water has few birds, although there may be Common Sandpipers in summer. Meadow Pipit is abundant, and watch for Raven passing along the skyline. Peregrine, Kestrel and Buzzard may be hunting along the slopes and tops, especially if the weather is kind.

2 A Buzzard, beating its way laboriously up from the south against a fierce northerly gale passed by me at head height, in the shelter from the crest; at the top, it suddenly gained the rising air rushing up the slopes, and instantly swept upwards on wide-spread wings, rocketing up hundreds of feet in moments.

3 At the top of the pass (splendid view down into the Kentmere Valley to the south), follow the ridge around the huge and gloomy cliffs above Blea Water. I witnessed a Golden Eagle 'stoop' down the sheer face in pursuit of a Raven which had been irritating it: close enough to hear the tearing sound of the wind through the feathers of the larger bird. On the rounded tops Ravens quarter the ground hoping to scavenge on the sandwich leavings of the tourists. Skylark is common, and you may see Wheatear where there are rocky slopes. In late April or early May, search for small 'trips' of Dotterel migrating north, sometimes stopping off to rest. Snow Bunting flocks are often present in winter.

4 It is possible to take a steep path down Long Stile along Riggindale Crag, but I recommend heading right around Riggindale, and up the far flanks to Kidsty Pike with its superb views down into Riggindale. Look for Red Deer couched far below.

5 If the Golden Eagles are nesting, the manned lookout (NY 464117) can be accessed from the obvious path running up the valley on the south side of the stream. Do not attempt any other approach: you risk disturbing the eagles (illegal if done wilfully – be warned!), and you will certainly have some justifiably angry wardens after you! The eagles might be seen at any time of year. They are most active early and late in the day, and may be seen circling the crags, or even soaring up and moving away to hunt elsewhere. Recent poor breeding success has suggested the birds are ageing; whether another pair will successfully emerge to replace them is uncertain.

6 On the walk back to the head of the reservoir look out for Greylag, Canada and (feral) Barnacle Geese, Cormorant, Red-breasted Merganser, Goosander and other ducks. Common Sandpiper and Grey Wagtail should be along the edges, and on the slopes may be Ring Ouzel, Redstart and Whinchat in summer, and Fieldfare in winter.

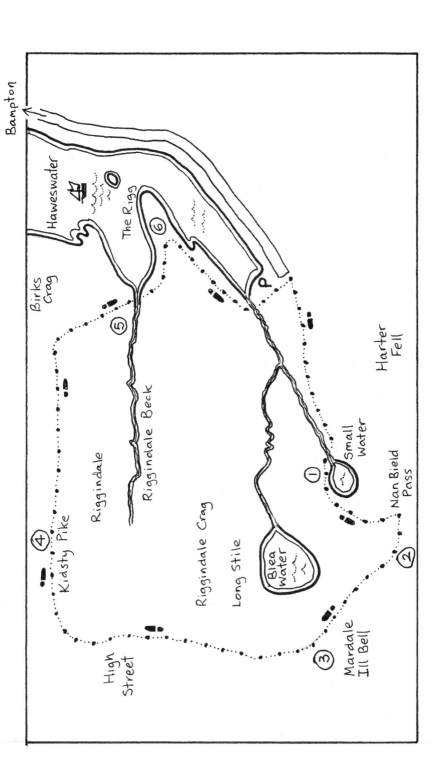

Bampton

Haweswater

Birks Crag

The Rigg

④

⑥

P

Harter Fell

Riggindale

Riggindale Beck

Small Water

Nan Bield Pass

①

Kidsty Pike

④

Riggindale Crag

Long Stile

Blea Water

②

High Street

Mardale Ill Bell

③

⑤

57

Place Fell & Ullswater

Start: Martindale Church   **Grid ref:** NY434184   **Distance:** 8½ miles/13.5 km
Maps: Landranger Sheet 90; Outdoor Leisure 5 *English Lakes (NE)*

A notably quiet corner of Lakeland, with fine views firstly up long glacier-carved valleys, then – at the col – a wide vista over Helvellyn and beyond to the Scafell range. It needs boots, but paths are mainly good. The route rises to over 500m (1640ft) at Bedafell Knott in a steady ascent. There is a short steep section on the path down from the col at Boardale Hause.

The best variety of birds in spring/summer (as described); winter can be very quiet.

1 The lower fellside pastures have abundant Meadow Pipit, with some Linnet and Yellowhammer. The rushy valley bottom should have a pair or two of Reed Bunting. Keep a lookout for Raven, Peregrine and Buzzard over the crags above.

2 At Dale Head, follow signs right for 'Patterdale'. The upper valleys of Ramps Gill and Bannerdale are perhaps the best place in Lakeland to see Red Deer, though they often merge surprisingly well into the bracken slopes: scan carefully with binoculars, using the sheep to give you the right sense of scale, and look for something very warm brown in colour: suddenly they should 'pop into view'!

  Snipe still occurs in the wet valley marshes, and more Reed Bunting pairs. Soon there are fine views up to the crags at the head of Bannerdale: listen for the piping song of Ring Ouzel in spring. Skylark will be singing above, with Wheatear families on the walls and Whinchat in the bracken.

3 On fine days flocks of Swift and House Martin ride the updrafts to feed on insects carried up to this height. Buzzard also hunts here. In summer Rooks bring their young up to these slopes to feast on the crane-fly hatchings. Don't be tempted to call these (nor the Carrion Crows) 'Ravens': Raven is much larger, rarer, and has a deep resonant *'kronk'* call. It seldom descends to the valley-bottom, but sails high like Buzzard.

4 Where there are woodlands below the path, check for both Pied and Spotted Flycatcher, Goldcrest, and the usual woodland Blackcap, Treecreeper, Willow Warbler, Song Thrush, Coal, Great and Blue Tit, etc. The mixed conifer wood just before the lake has many good birds: Tawny Owl, Siskin, Redstart, Nuthatch and Cuckoo.

5 The reed-fringed bay has Coot and Mallard, with Common Sandpiper and Grey Heron. The wonderful juniper/birch woods from here onwards alongside the lake have numerous Goldcrest, Robin and Willow Warbler. There are usually at least three Tree Pipit territories along the slopes above the path to the north.

6 At the tarmac, turn right, then follow the stream and track to 'Bridgend' and 'Swinsty'. Then turn left at a 'Public Bridleway' sign, up a narrow 'green lane', through a barn-yard, across the stream, and keep right back to the start. Redstart nests along here with Willow Warbler, and Linnets should be flighting over.

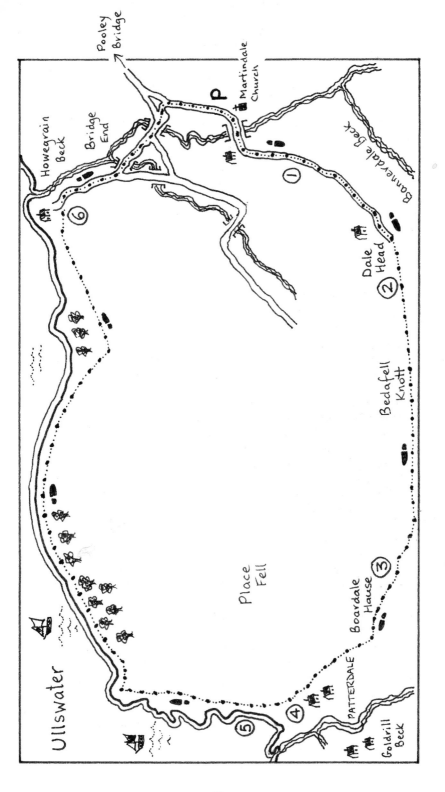

Ullswater

Pooley Bridge

Martindale Church

P

Bannerdale Beck

Howegrain Beck

Bridge End

① Dale Head ②

⑥

Bedafell Knott

Place Fell

Boardale Hause ③

PATTERDALE ④

⑤

Goldrill Beck

Gowbarrow & Swinburn's Park

Start: Aira Force NT car-park **Grid ref:** NY401201 **Distance:** 7½ miles/12 km
Maps: Landranger Sheet 90; Outdoor Leisure 5 *English Lakes (NE)*

A reasonably level walk, with grand views over Ullswater and Place Fell, then Matterdale, with Blencathra behind. Stout footware is required. The NT car-park at Aira Force is free to NT members, or walk from Dockray. The parking area has wonderfully tame Nuthatch, Chaffinch and tits which will come readily to food in your hand (at least early in the day, before they get satiated!).

1 Follow the tourists to the bridge over Aira Beck, where Nuthatch is again often prominent, and a couple of hundred metres up the far bank fork right, with a wooden fence on your right. Cross the fence at a stile a little further on, by a huge old stump, and then take the level path across the fell-side. Above curious 'Lyulph's Tower' fork left up the slope of Gowbarrow, across open fell-slope with bracken and scattered trees, perfect for Tree Pipit in summer. Buzzard and Peregrine have territories in the neighbourhood: keep an eye open for these, but keep the other on the path!

2 Enjoy the superb view from the large cairn at the top of Yew Crag, then fork left up the oblique path (sheets of flowering Bell-heather in summer), and round to the north until you see the huge 'saucer' of Swinburn's Park opening up before you.

3 In winter scan for Greylag Geese in the fields towards the lake; Fieldfare should be in the Hawthorns. Ring Ouzel may be in the same trees in early spring soon after its arrival. Meadow Pipit is abundant in season, and Whinchat too in the bracken – listen for the thin wispy song, easily missed.

4 Contour along, forking right at the ruined shooting hut, and enter the new forestry by the stile. Redpoll and Siskin winter in mixed flocks, feasting on the alder 'cones', and the former also summers here. Fieldfare and Redwing join resident Mistle and Song Thrushes in winter, and there will always be tits, Goldcrest and Treecreeper.

5 After Gate Crags, you will drop down into farmland again; steer left of the rectory, and back to the road north of the church. Mistle Thrush sings here from January onwards in mild weather – a glorious ringing fluty song.

6 Turn left up the hill, and cross The Hause between Priest Crag and Little Mell Fell.

7 Turn left again following the sign for Ulcat Row. There are still some good rough fields here, and with luck Curlew and Lapwing, with Yellowhammer in the hedges.

8 At the bottom of the hill, opposite 'Undercrag', follow the wooden sign for Dockray and Aira Force along a delightful 'green lane', right round below steep Norman Crag as far as Millses Mill, where a three-way sign (9) directs you south towards Aira Force. Soon you drop into the Aira valley, and you can stop off to look at the spectacular falls, and return to the car-park down paths on either side of the water. Dipper is on quieter stretches, and tit flocks in the trees. Besides many Coot, Ullswater may have Mallard and Tufted Duck and rarer grebes in its quieter bays – Slavonian Grebe has been a recent winterer.

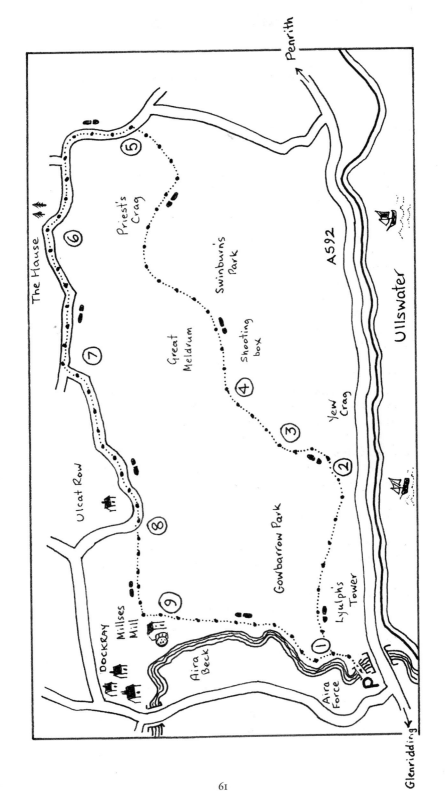

Penrith

The Hause

Priest's Crag

Swinburn's Park

A592

Ullswater

Great Meldrum

Shooting box

Yew Crag

Ulcat Row

Gowbarrow Park

Lyulph's Tower

DOCKRAY

Millses Mill

Aira Beck

Aira Force

P

Glenridding

① ② ③ ④ ⑤ ⑥ ⑦ ⑧ ⑨

Thirlmere & Watendlath Fell

Start: Dob Gill car-park   **Grid ref:** NY316140   **Distance:** 8 miles/13 km
Maps: Landranger Sheet 90; Outdoor Leisure 5 *English Lakes (NE)*

A very varied landscape of forest, sheltered and exposed tarns, wild moorland, with spectacular views on to Helvellyn to the east, and all the western fells. The moors can be very boggy: good high boots or even wellingtons are likely to be needed to keep dry feet! Best in summer; the fells tops are very quiet in winter.

Starting from the Dob Gill car-park (don't leave valuables in a vehicle, nor anything tempting in view), follow the track up into the plantations of spruce, pine and larch, with their typical avian inhabitants: Coal Tit and other tits, Siskin, Goldcrest, and abundant Willow Warbler, Chaffinch and Robin. Harrop Tarn is very delightful with its sheltered situation and wooded backdrops – on a sunny day, reckon to tarry a long while here! Mallard, Coot, Grey Heron, Grey Wagtail are likely, and Little Grebe often nests here. Buzzard and Raven are often over the stern crags beyond. Keep straight up the bridleway signed to 'Watendlath' to the right of the stream, and after a further 100m follow blue arrows up to the right – a rocky path heading up the slope from the forestry track. The upper levels of the forest are beech, perfect for Wood Warbler. At times the singing bird is so engrossed in its song as to ignore the observer. There are two different songs: the more frequent is a stunning accelerating 'shivery trill', one of the most evocative sounds of the upland hanging woods. The other, utterly different, is interspersed at intervals between the trills, and is a loud, descending, tuneful, *'piu, piu, piu, piu, piu, ...'*.

1 Look out for Raven, Buzzard and Kestrel over the open fell (loud cries of indignation from the Carrion Crows often signal the presence of birds of prey!). In summer, Skylark and Meadow Pipit are common all over the moor, and Cuckoo may be calling from the valley sides where there are a few hawthorns.

2 The view over the hamlet of Watendlath is spectacular, and you could drop down to visit it for refreshments. You lose a lot of height, however, which will have to be regained as you struggle back up again! Watch for Tree Pipit and Redstart on the slopes below. Turn right here and head straight up the hill towards High Tove, from where the path drops down again into the Thirlmere valley.

3 Snipe nest in some of the little boggy swamps on the slopes as you descend. Take care on the steep and rocky path down Fisher Gill to Armboth, back on to tarmac.

4 In the steep wooded slopes above the road is an excellent variety of birds in summer, including Pied Flycatcher, Tree Pipit, Wood Warbler (as well as many more of the related Willow Warbler), Blackcap, Redstart, Great Spotted Woodpecker, several tit species, Goldcrest and Siskin. Common Sandpiper occurs along the water's edge. Keep a close eye on the sky at all times: you may see a Peregrine swooping and playing around Buzzards along the higher cliffs. Ferns in great abundance, variety and vigour – at least twenty species – are a feature of the roadside banks and woods.

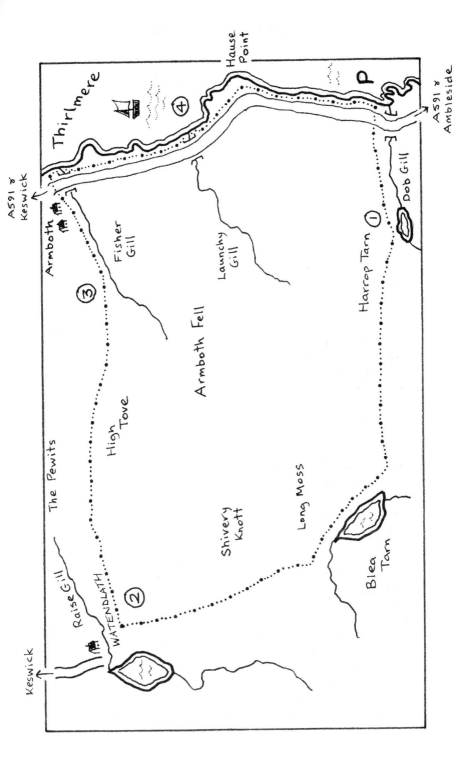

Derwent Water

Start: Keswick (Launch jetty) **Grid ref:** NY264227 **Distance:** 9 miles/14.5 km
Maps: Landranger Sheet 90; Outdoor Leisure 4 *English Lakes (NW)*

There are so many possibilities here that you can choose your own route and distance!
The great boon for walkers is the launch service around the lake; launches run both
ways round the lake, and call in at several points – anti-clockwise, they are Keswick,
Nichol End, Hawes End, Low and High Brandlehow, Lodore, Ashness Gate. Pick up
a leaflet with the current timings at the Keswick jetty, any tourist information bureau
in the area, or the office of the Derwent Water Launch Co. (29 Manor Park, Keswick),
or phone 017687 72263. You could walk the quieter western shore, and cruise back to
your base from any point on the south or east shore, or cruise first to your preferred
start and walk back. The paths are all good, although the eastern shore path follows
the lakeside gravel for much of the way, which can be rough in places.

1 The northern bays are somewhat infested with Mallard, with an admixture of
   domestic stock, making for a few oddly patterned birds. There are also a few pairs
   of apparently wild-living, black-and-white Muscovy Duck around the lake. However,
   both Goosander and Red-breasted Merganser nest, and you might see broods of
   ducklings of either species in summer. Reed Bunting sings in the marshes at the
   bay-head.

2 The Lingholm woods have an excellent mix of woodland birds: Nuthatch, Goldcrest,
   Treecreeper; several tit species including Long-tailed and Coal; Mistle and Song
   Thrush; Redstart in summer.

3 Brandlehow: Redstart is also in most of the other woods around the lake: watch
   for them flashing across your path to feed young in holes in the oaks right next to
   the lake. Common Sandpiper has a few pairs along quieter bays.

4 The open country above Brandlehow Bay has Yellowhammer and Meadow Pipit.
   There are often tame pairs of Red-breasted Merganser in the bay, constantly 'peeking'
   under the water in search of food. They like feeding in the shallow water over gravel
   beds. This is a superb bird to watch closely, with its long, slender, red 'saw-bill'.

5 Pines in Manesty Park attract Crossbills on occasion, and the open areas have Tree
   Pipit, Redpoll, feeding Swift; when seeding, the birches tempt out Siskins from the
   woods. They can feed unobtrusively until suddenly flushing out and away.

6 The southern bays have many Canada Geese, but the Greylag Goose has colonised
   the lake in a most impressive fashion: in June/July there are moulting flocks of
   several hundred along south and east shores. These are also the best areas in winter
   when there are always many diving ducks to be seen – Goldeneye, Pochard, Tufted
   Duck – and sometimes rare grebes and divers, especially Great Northern, along with
   Black-headed and Common Gulls and Coot.

7 Wood Warbler and Pied Flycatcher are in the steep oak woods here in summer,
   and the usual mixture of Great, Blue, Long-tailed and Coal Tits.

8 Keep a lookout for Peregrine along the crags before and above Great Wood.

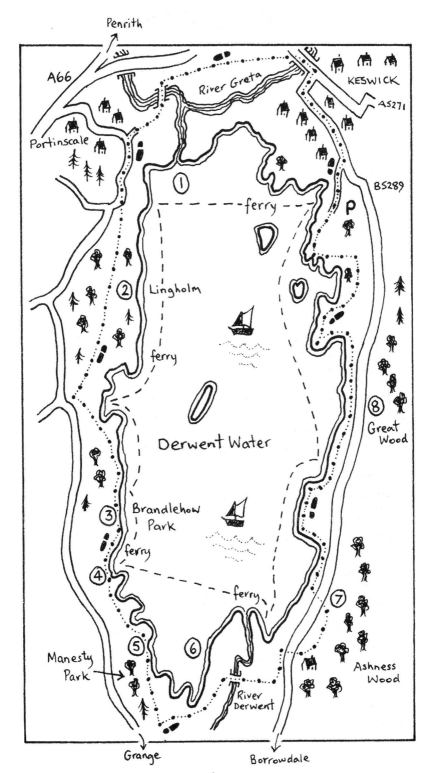

Buttermere

Start: Buttermere (village) **Grid ref:** NY175170 **Distance:** 5 miles/8 km
Maps: Landranger Sheets 89 or 90; Outdoor Leisure 4 *English Lakes (NW)*

A much more benign walk than that around Crummock Water: it is shorter, the paths are through woodland for much of the way and are in generally better repair. However, it is for these reasons much more popular, and in summer you will find it more difficult to get away from other folks for your birding. Nonetheless, it is a delightful walk in superb scenery, and perhaps because of the numbers of walkers, the birds are generally tame and approachable. Best in spring and summer, and early morning will avoid the crowds.

The official car-parks at Buttermere village and at Gatesgarth are expensive: you will however see folks parking in several other places along the road.

1 The view across the valley on to the 'hanging' oakwoods is sublime in spring, when the yellow-brown fluffy rounded tops of the oaks contrast with the deeper green of the birches.

2 Cut down directly to the landing stage, or even better, cross to Scale Bridge, and enjoy the superbly clear water in Buttermere Dubs. Watch for Dipper, usually rushing past calling loudly.

3 The lakeside path through Burtness Wood gives fine views across to the Newlands hills opposite, but is busy; the upper path is quiet, and in summer you should be able to get perfect views – and sounds – of singing Tree Pipit where the woods are more open. It likes to sing from the tops of tall trees next to this upper path, and its glorious loud song cascades around the slopes. The song is even better when there is another bird singing further up the slope to provide some competition. Listen also for Redstart and Pied Flycatcher, the former more frequent. Wood Warbler is in several places in the mixed woodland; song and habitat complement each other perfectly. Other woodland birds here are Treecreeper, Goldcrest, Coal Tit, Mistle Thrush and abundant Willow Warbler. Scan for Raven and Buzzard along the cliff tops. Common Sandpiper and Pied Wagtail are among the few birds which like the shingle shores.

4 Follow the permissive path along the lakeshore. There should be several pairs of Red-breasted Merganser; they can be amazingly tame, and will dive so close to shore you may be able to follow them underwater by the flash of white in their wings. Goosander is also present but less common.

5 The woods here are more varied, and again listen for Redstart, Wood Warbler and Pied Flycatcher amongst the noisy thrushes, Wren, Chaffinch and Willow Warbler.

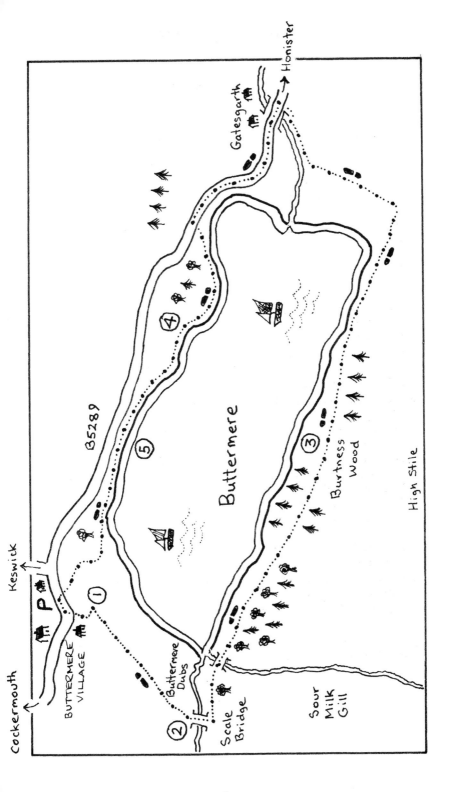

Cockermouth

Keswick

Buttermere Village

B5289

Buttermere

Buttermere Dubs

Scale Bridge

Sour Milk Gill

Burtness Wood

High Stile

Gatesgarth

Honister

① ② ③ ④ ⑤

Crummock Water

Start: Cinderdale   **Grid ref:** NY162194   **Distance:** 7½ miles/12 km
Maps: Landranger Sheet 89; Outdoor Leisure 4 *English Lakes (NW)*

Park as above, or at any of the other numerous lay-bys. The path is obvious, but wet at times, and rocky in places. This is quite a long and arduous walk. Do not underestimate the energy needed to do the full circuit. There is much more to see in the bird-line in summer, as in most of the description below, except perhaps for variety of waterfowl.

1 Open ground has Yellowhammer and Cuckoo, with both Whinchat and Stonechat on the bracken-dominated slopes above. In the mixed woods beyond, listen for Wood Warbler along with more frequent Chiffchaff and Willow Warbler. Garden Warbler also nests, and there are the usual woodland Long-tailed and Coal Tits, Goldcrest and Treecreeper. Great Spotted Woodpecker and Jay occur regularly.

2 Cross the lake outlet by the footbridges, then south along the west shore: the path is poor in places, but you can follow the shingle unless the lake is high. Reed Bunting is in the rushy meadows, and the shore has Common Sandpiper, Pied Wagtail, and at times Grey Heron. Stonechat is usually around the slopes above. It can be surprisingly difficult to spot the bird after you have located its distinctive call, 'like two stones knocked together'. Meadow Pipit is everywhere abundant.

3 Goosander, Cormorant and Great Crested Grebe may be out on the water, and a variety of diving ducks in winter, of which Goldeneye is often the most obvious. Watch out for Peregrine following any of the cliffs on either side of the valley. If you fail to spot this much-celebrated species, it is likely to be because the bird can be very inconspicuous if perched on the crags, or when soaring at a great height overhead. Kestrel and Buzzard should also be present on most occasions.

4 Goldcrest abounds in some autumns in the isolated bushes across the alluvial fan of the Scale Beck. You can walk up to Scale Waterfall by way of a diversion. Dipper should be seen along here at any time of year.

5 The superb hanging oakwoods above the path along to Scale Bridge have all the expected specialities in summer: Wood Warbler, Pied Flycatcher, Redstart, as well as woodland species mentioned already.

6 Cut across the valley to Buttermere village; you are walking across a 'bridge' of material washed down by the Mill Beck over the thousands of years since the Ice Age, dividing the original glacial lake into what is now two. Follow the road for a quarter of a mile, looping above the road along the track through Great Wood, then on rejoining the lakeshore, look for the path which rises above the road past Hause Point. Crossing Rannerdale, the right-of-way actually curves across the head of the valley (as marked), and then brings you back to the start. If you have insufficient strength by now, simply stick to the road, which is unfortunately walled-in at this point.

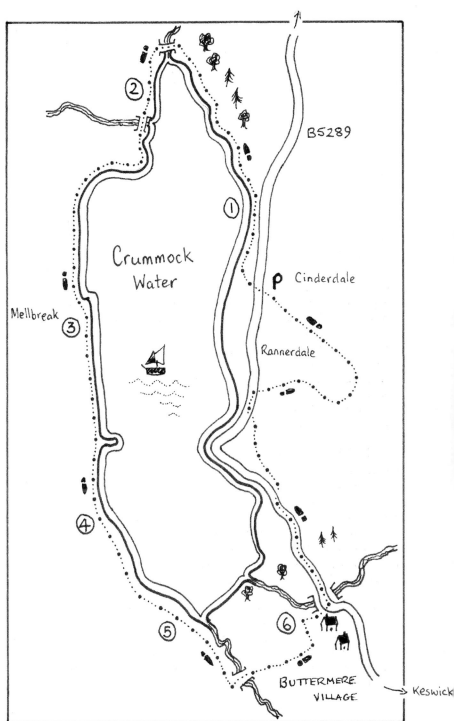

Cockermouth

B5289

②

①

Crummock
Water

P   Cinderdale

Mellbreak

③

Rannerdale

④

⑤

⑥

BUTTERMERE
VILLAGE

→ Keswick

Workington & Siddick Pond

Start: Workington   **Grid ref:** NX990298   **Distance:** 3½ miles/5.5 km
Maps: Landranger Sheet 89; Pathfinder 583 (NX92, NX93, NY02 & NY03)

Something to be seen at all times of the year. Good tracks.

1 At the junction of the A596 and A597, turn west down a road signed 'The Docks' (NX999296), and then after a quarter of a mile, turn right (north) at the sign for a camp-site and caravan-site. The next left takes you to a cliff-top park just north of the docks, or drive north: lots of places to park next to the coast and walk. On the sea watch for Cormorant, divers, grebes, gulls including Kittiwake, and passing terns in season. The docks area to the south may have nesting Ringed Plover, and check gull roosts: a Ross's Gull has been recorded in the past.

2 Walk north and search the fields and hedges on all sides. Whitethroat and Willow Warbler are common, and Rock Pipit is present as well as Meadow Pipit, and abundant Skylark. In spring and autumn, look out for migrant Wheatear and Whinchat, warblers and finches. Linnet and Stonechat can be seen all year. The beach has nesting Ringed Plover and Oystercatcher, and Redshank and Turnstone in winter.

3 Cross the A597 and aim for a gap in the long wooden fence at NX999299. This cuts through between the allotments to the ponds.

4 This saline pool has Mute Swan, Coot and Moorhen, and scrub around the edge has Sedge Warbler and Stonechat.

5 The old railway gives excellent views over Siddick Pond itself. In summer, you can look down on singing Reed Warbler, Sedge Warbler, and possible Reed Bunting. (Reed Warbler seems to be expanding northwards, and is now well-established here.) Coot and Moorhen are abundant – feeding their ridiculous-looking young – and check carefully for Little Grebe among the Tufted Duck and Pochard flocks. Pochard and Shoveler nest. Teal and Wigeon are often on show in winter, and Grey Heron and Cormorant are usually present. The resident Mute Swans are joined in winter by Whooper Swan, sometimes in numbers. Rarer visitors have included Bearded Tit (the reed-beds look big enough for this species to colonise), Garganey, Marsh Harrier and Little Gull. A Bittern spent several winters here. I once flushed a Quail from the edge in mid-June. Cross the A596 by the bridge, and double under it to regain the path.

6 The hide you can see at the northern end is available for public use: go into Iggesund Paper Board's main entrance, and ask for the key at the security building.

7 With the advent of wind-turbines, wintering Golden Plover and Lapwing now tend to use the shore and other less-disturbed fields. Small birds can still be seen, however.

8 Cross the railway line with care, and walk south along the coast, keeping a good look out to sea for passing flocks of waders and ducks. Fine Sea Kale on the beach: masses of white flower in June.

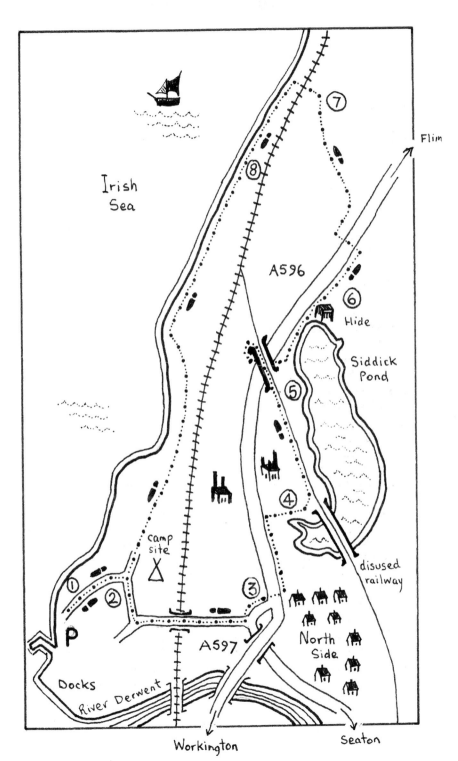

Irish
Sea

Flim

⑦

⑧

A596

⑥
Hide

Siddick
Pond

⑤

④

disused
railway

camp
site

① ② ③

North
Side

P

A597

Docks
River Derwent

Workington

Seaton

71

Mungrisdale & Bannerdale

Start: Mungrisdale   **Grid ref:** NY362303   **Distance:** 7½ miles/12 km
Maps: Landranger Sheet 90; Outdoor Leisure 5 *English Lakes (NE)*

Delightful walking: grassy tracks, general lack of bogs, few walkers, and a sense of solitude lacking elsewhere. Many possible routes: consult your map. The circuit described here has steady ascents and descents, with easy routes off the hill, if conditions demand. However, if clouds are down, do not set out without compass and prayers: the plateau is confusing in mist, and ends suddenly in steep – or vertical! – slopes in several directions.

As to be expected in this sort of country, the variety of birds is not high, but the enjoyment of birds in such grand country should be savoured. Late April and May are recommended.

1 If parking in the village you may be asked to contribute a fee in some of the available spots. While booting-up, listen for Grey and Pied Wagtail by the stream, Whitethroat in the gorse and Whinchat in the bracken. On the gravel track heading west, listen for Redstart in the trees in the gorge just up from the bridge.

2 Cross the wooden footbridge, and take the *right-hand* track rising steeply, passing to the left of the cliffs ('The Tongue'). I have heard Willow Warbler in song in the juniper bushes here at about 1400 feet. Is it only a migrant at this altitude? See how far up the valley you can track Wrens by their insistent songs. Whinchat will be in the bracken below the cliffs, and from here on up you will seldom be out of the sound of singing Wheatear and Meadow Pipit.

3 Look out for Kestrel and Buzzard hanging over the flanks as you slog up Bannerdale. Best, however, is the cascade of song from dozens of Skylarks taking advantage of the up-draughts. At the head of Bannerdale, the rather mournful piping song of the Ring Ouzel should be ringing around the corrie. Actually seeing the bird will entail more time, and some luck!

4 At the saddle, various options open up. Turn right for Bowscale Fell (2306 feet). Rounded short turf tops like this might attract passing Dotterel from late April to early May: you may be lucky, but they can be remarkably inconspicuous, being tame and undemonstrative. Your best hope is to catch them silhouetted against the skyline. Now back to the head of Bannerdale and round, for spectacular views over the cliffs. Raven should be soaring above or below you, but remember that Carrion Crow can ascend this high, and on warm summer days Rooks come up for the crane-fly hatches. Peregrine should be somewhere to be seen.

5 Drop down to the obvious col (NY328292). The summit of Blencathra is another 600 feet above and can be attempted if you have time, and steam. Otherwise, enjoy the view, as you follow the path which drops down into the V-shaped valley of the Glenderamackin. Follow the river right back down to Mungrisdale.

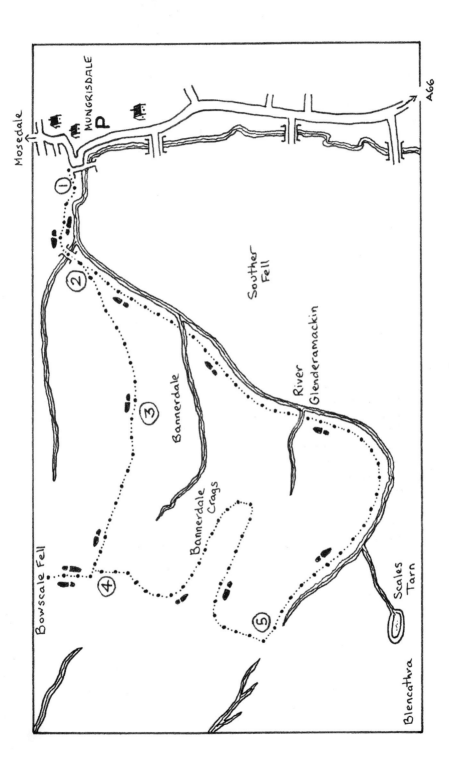

Askham & River Lowther

Start: Askham village green **Grid ref:** NY515237 **Distance:** 5½ miles/9 km
Maps: Landranger Sheet 90; Outdoor Leisure 5 *English Lakes (NE)*

This walk in the fringes of the Lake District is set in limestone country, and has almost the atmosphere of the Pennine Dales. Being in the rain-shadow of the Lakeland hills here, you may well find it a retreat from a wet day in the central Lakes.

1 Park by the village green and walk down the hill to Askham Bridge. In summer, listen for Blackcap and other warblers, and scan the river for Dipper and Goosander, both of which you may see anywhere along the Lowther.

2 The mixed plantations are full of tits, Treecreeper and Goldcrest all year, and Great Spotted Woodpecker and Sparrowhawk are frequent enough. After a few hundred yards you burst out of the woods to get a superb view of the upper river valley.

3 On a good day Buzzards often drift along the scarp on your left – my best count is eight at once! – and Kestrel, Sparrowhawk and Goshawk may also appear (in declining order of likelihood). Even a Raven sometimes keeps an eye on things from the rising air over the cliffs.

4 When the river bends away from you towards Crookwath Bridge, you can regain the main road and shorten the trip, or continue through the lowest edge of the mixed plantation ahead of you (good for woodland birds and Red Squirrel) following the wayposts out of the wood at the far end.

5 Cross the paddock (*not* through the farmyard), and back to the road, via a wicket gate atop four steps in the wall ahead. The little hamlet of Whale has Swallow in season, Mistle Thrush, and some superb drystone walling.

Somewhere in the fields, in winter, you should find a large or small mass of Greylag Geese, apparently the now-wild descendants of released birds of native Scottish origin. Check through the flock for (escaped) Bar-headed, Snow, and other geese.

6 Cross the main road and follow Whale Beck down to the Lowther footbridge. It is a lovely walk back north along the west side of the river, well-marked. We saw singing Redstart, Pied and Grey Wagtail, several pairs of Common Sandpiper, Goosander, Sand Martin, Bullfinch, and many others.

7 Walk north along the (quiet) road for about a kilometre, to a stile on the right, just before the junction. This leads back to the village church and Askham Bridge.

8 If you have time, and after refreshment, you can take the 'northern loop' by crossing over the river again, up the hill and through parkland past the amazing northern aspect of Lowther Castle, to a right-of-way running north (9), down to two bridges (10), one old and one new, over the Lowther. Many good birds are also here, with more chances of Dipper and Grey and Pied Wagtails. Turn left after the bridge, and a footpath brings you up and out of the woods, and back into Askham from the north.

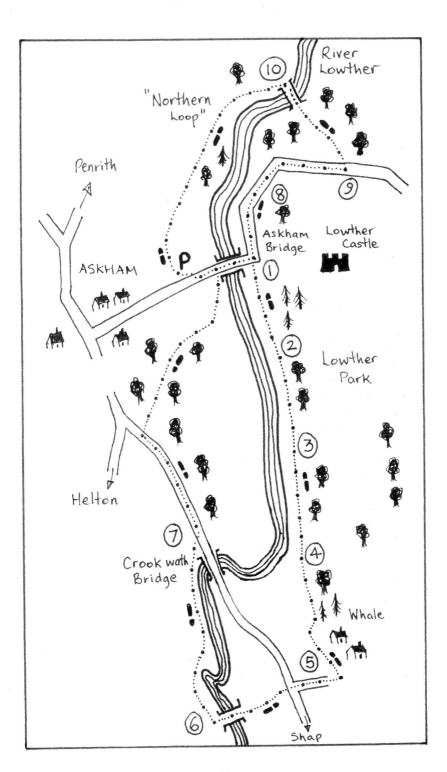

River Lowther

"Northern Loop"

Penrith

ASKHAM

P

Askham Bridge

Lowther Castle

Lowther Park

Helton

Crook wath Bridge

Whale

Shap

Kirkby Thore & Upper River Eden

Start: Bolton village   **Grid ref:** NY637233   **Distance:** 5 miles/8 km
Maps: Landranger Sheet 91; Pathfinder NY62

A pleasant easy walk along lanes and through fields, to the middle Eden. Best in summer. You may park in Bolton village – there are stretches of wide road by the Memorial Hall and playground – or walk from Kirkby Thore: there is a conveniently-situated lay-by on the westbound side of the A66 just east of the village.

1 Follow Broadings Lane past Bolton Hall right to its end. The overgrown hedges with trees have Redstart and Whitethroat, with Yellowhammer in places. Many pairs of Oystercatcher in the fields, now well outnumbering the Curlew and Lapwing which have not tolerated the drainage of wet fields and resowing of grasslands.

2 The little marshy corner here, and the scrubby willows beyond, have a small population of very mimetic Sedge Warblers: see what bird-calls you can recognise in their songs. I heard perfect renditions of Swallow, Great Tit and Goldfinch.

3 Another way to point 2 is to walk west from Bolton past Mansgrove to NY624234 and take Crossrigg Lane to Peatgate, where a footpath cuts across fields to the river. Again, listen out for Whitethroat along the hedges.

4 At Ousenstand Bridge start back upstream on the north side, following the river-bank all the way to Kirkby Thore. Common Sandpiper is frequent and Sand Martin abundant. Redshank still appears to breed, although there are few swampy spots left in the resown fields; there are several pairs.

5 Where there are deeper stretches, Tufted Duck is likely in winter, and seems to be colonising as a nester too. Other waterfowl are Goosander, many Mallard, and one or two pairs of Mute Swan, nesting on quieter stretches.

6 Aim for a footbridge over Trout Beck (NY635252), then cling to the stream and river banks. Or follow signs into the village, cross the stream by the main road bridge, and look out for a footpath sign saying, ominously, "Bolton by deep ford" – the ford part doesn't apply to you! Along the river will be Pied Wagtail and in summer, with luck, the odd Yellow Wagtail, certainly Moorhen, and more Common Sandpiper. Sand Martin nests where the riparian owners have not dumped rubble onto the banks in an attempt to arrest erosion. One May I saw two Twite bathing here: they are very late migrants to their mountain nesting areas.

7 In the scrub look out for Long-tailed and other tits, and listen for Blackcap amongst the more frequent Willow Warbler.

8 In winter look out for Siskin and Redpoll in the alders, and in summer, Goldfinch and Linnet. Gently crush the leaves of Sweet Cicely – the white-flowered 'parsley' here – for a delicious fragrance of aniseed, and the leaves of the yellow-flowered Tansy for a mind-blowing smell of menthol.

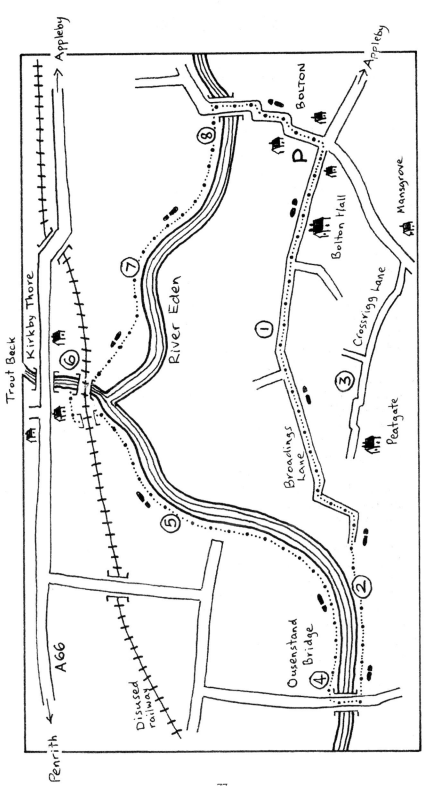

Cross Fell

Start: Kirkland   **Grid ref:** NY650325   **Distance:** 10 miles/16 km

Maps: Landranger Sheet 91; Outdoor Leisure 31 *Teesdale & Weardale*

Mileage given above is for the longer way through Blencarn.

Choose a clear day for this walk: it is very easy indeed to get lost on the featureless tops in mist – as I have myself done – and then miss your route on the way down. It is long and rough: good boots and fitness essential. Very few birds to be seen in winter, although you may see Snow Bunting flocks then. Dotterel passage is very irregular: I have seen them on less than half my many visits to the tops in the passage season (most likely late-April to mid-May). The joy of watching this most exquisite bird more than compensates for the failures! Please stick to the paths on the tops, and do not attract attention to the birds if you find them. Sit quietly, and you may have close views. The birds are often in the vicinity of the path along the top of the ridge, often a few yards on the lee side (protected from the wind), whichever side that is at the time.

From Kirkland walk up the track on to the fell. Swift and House Martin nest in the village, and Pied Flycatcher and Redstart are in the first clough (small wooded valley) beyond. Next your path crosses the Kirkland Beck, where there is gorse with Linnet, Whinchat, Yellowhammer and Reed Bunting in summer, and of course abundant Skylark and Meadow Pipit.

1 As you skirt round the lower escarpments look out for Buzzard and Raven soaring along the ridges. Snipe and Golden Plover nest on the flat moor beyond, and at higher levels a few pairs of Dunlin occur. For some unexplained reason a single Dunlin will often follow a single Golden Plover around, so it is worth looking closely at all perched Plovers for this otherwise inconspicuous bird.

2 Do not be tempted to aim for the summit of Cross Fell too soon! Keep to the path up on to the northwest flank of the summit, when you see the proper path – the Pennine Way – up the stony shoulder.

3 Dotterel will only be on the highest slopes or summits, where the turf is very sparse. Flocks often rest up in clumps of Heath Rush, and are then extremely inconspicuous. Very patient scanning with binoculars might bring rewards. They do not seem to try to avoid the many walkers attracted to this highest Pennine 'top', and I have seen them on several occasions roosting quietly within yards of the Pennine Way. There may also be Golden Plover on the summit, so avoid jubilation when you spot distant plovers on the skyline, until you can check for the features of the Dotterel! Other birds on the flat top are Wheatear, Skylark, Meadow Pipit, and occasional Dunlin.

4 Follow the Pennine Way off the southeast flank, and pick up the bridleway above Crowdundle Beck at NY696339, and down the long descent into Blencarn. Through the village, turn right and back up the fell to Kirkland, checking the pool on the right.

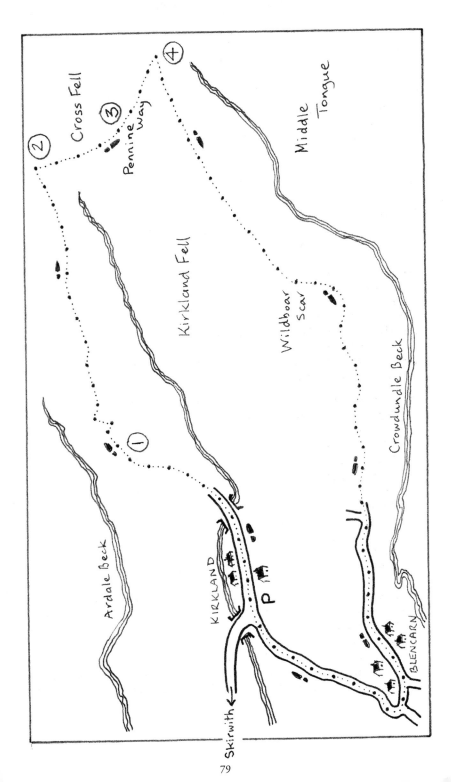

Ardale Beck

Cross Fell

② ③ ④

Pennine Way

Kirkland Fell

Middle Tongue

Wildboar Scar

①

Crowdundle Beck

KIRKLAND

P

Skirwith

BLENCARN

Garrigill & South Tynedale

Start: Garrigill village   **Grid ref:** NY744416   **Distance:** 5 miles/8 km
Maps: Landranger Sheet 86; Outdoor Leisure 31 *Teesdale & Weardale*

Much richer in summer than at other times, and being at an altitude of over 1000 feet, can be expected to have a limited selection of birds in winter. Very scenic riverside walk. Mostly a good path, but can be muddy in places.

1 Park in the village of Garrigill and walk out along the south side of the river to the footpath sign. Pied and Grey Wagtail can be seen where the river flows through the village, as well as anywhere along the river. Spotted Flycatcher, Greenfinch and Goldfinch can all be seen around the village, with Willow Warbler and Blackcap in the scrub beyond. Jackdaw is abundant both nesting in the village, and foraging in the short-turf fields by the river, often with Rook. Carrion Crow is also common.

2 Now follow the riverside path downstream, with Common Sandpiper and Dipper along the stream, and Oystercatcher and Curlew in the fields. Listen for Tree Pipit song where there are trees to act as song-perches. The river gravels here are well-known to be contaminated by lead, both naturally-occurring, and as a result of past lead-mining. The presence of lead-tolerant plants like Mountain Pansy, Thrift, Spring Sandwort and other specialised plants is due to the suppressing effect of the lead on ranker competing plants.

3 Several paths run through the birches to the wooden footbridge over Rotherhope Cleugh. Garden Warbler is as frequent as Blackcap in these scrubby areas. Willow Warbler should be abundant in summer, with other birds of open woodland such as Stock Dove (which is as likely to nest in isolated old barns in the fields as in hollow trees). Keep an eye open for Buzzard soaring along the ridges opposite; Rough-legged Buzzard is also occasionally sighted in the area in winters when there has been an 'arrival' of these erratic and spasmodic visitors from Scandinavia. Kestrel and Sparrowhawk should also be present, the former fluttering over the slopes, especially where there is some rougher grass or bracken, and the latter mostly keeping low, and dashing between the copses in the hope of surprising its prey.

4 Cross the main river, and follow a sign on the right to 'Meadow Flatt'. Blue-on-yellow signs zigzag up the hill, until the Pennine Way sign. If you follow this, it takes you back to another bridge back across the river, and back the way you came. To return to Garrigill, follow the sign as indicated up the hill, and follow the top of the woods. The path is then well-marked back to Garrigill, coming out eventually on the road just before the village.

5 Tree Pipit and Redstart will be among the birds to be seen in the woodland edges, and listen for Pied Flycatcher. Tawny Owl will be calling in winter evenings, though often very inconspicuous at other times. Redpoll is also present.

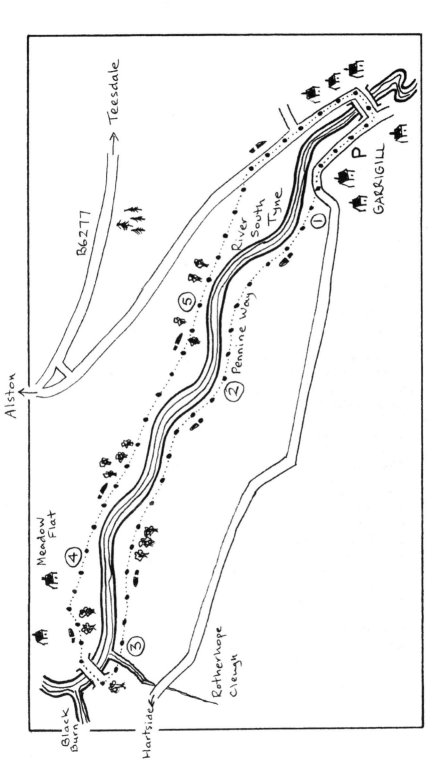

Teesdale

B6277

Alston

Garrigill

P

River South Tyne

Pennine Way

Meadow Flat

Black Burn

Hartside

Rotherhope Cleugh

① ② ③ ④ ⑤

River Petteril & Wreay Woods

Start: picnic site   **Grid ref:** NY435513   **Distance:** 4 miles/6.5 km
Maps: Landranger Sheet 85; Pathfinder 558 & 568 (NY44 & NY45)

A pleasant river-walk close to Carlisle. Further down the Petteril, paths follow the river right into the city if you want to extend the walk. Best in spring and summer.

1 Park in the picnic area by the M6 just west of junction 42 on the Dalston road. Follow yellow waymarkers into the field before the old stone bridge; then upriver and under the motorway. I once watched a Moorhen distracting a stoat from its chicks here. Grey Wagtail occurs, and Oystercatcher nests in the fields in spring.

2 Look for Siskin in the alders in winter: the birds may be very unobtrusive, and even quite large flocks can sit quietly feeding above your head unseen, until suddenly they start out, when their shrill twittering gives them away. A few Redpoll may be with them. Both Dipper and Kingfisher should be visible, though generally briefly as they speed away.

3 Wreay Woods (Wreay is pronounced 'Ree-ah' locally) is a Cumbria Wildlife Trust reserve. The first part, alongside the river, is often muddy, but take heart as further upstream the path rises higher on the valley side. Long-tailed Tit is often the commonest tit, but look also for Marsh Tit and the other species. Great Spotted Woodpecker, Goldcrest and usually Buzzard are to be seen all through the year; Blackcap, Garden Warbler, Chiffchaff and other warblers in summer. Sparrowhawk should be visible, although sometimes only given away by the loud alarms of the smaller birds, especially the sharp-eyed tits.

4 Past a large rookery across the river. Listen all along here for the rather shorter and throatier 'oou-oo' (i.e. two syllables) of Stock Dove, amongst the loud and persistent 'oo-ooo-oo, oo-oo' of Woodpigeon (five syllables in two groups).

5 Follow the waymarkers across the green iron bridge, up the far side, and then diagonally up to a lane which leads left into Wreay village (pub and shops). Back at the main road turn right. Look for the large Swift colonies around the rather odd buildings on the left as you head north out of the village. Spotted Flycatcher and Goldfinch are frequent around the village in summer.

6 After Low Hirst maintenance compound, take footpath signs to 'Golden Fleece' on the right towards the motorway, then north along the railway edge: there are even some Spotted Orchids in the stream-sides here. A set-aside field here had at least six pairs of Lapwing recently, greatly boosting their numbers locally, but only in the short-term.

7 Cross the railway by the bridge, and at Newbiggin Hall turn left for a short stretch out onto the Dalston/Golden Fleece road, then turn right back to the start.

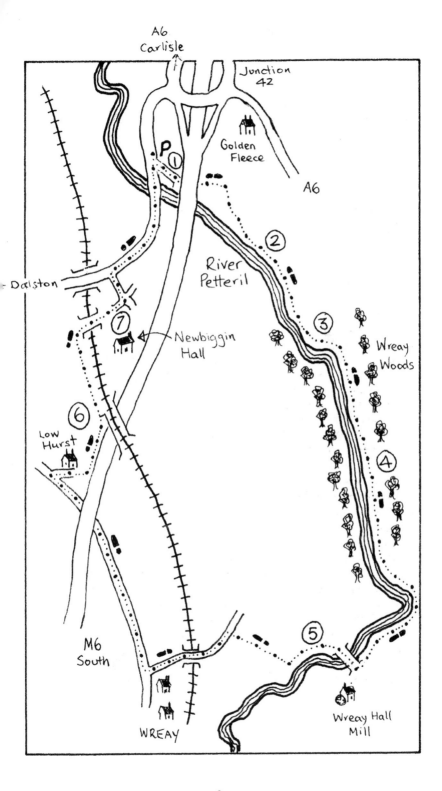

A6
Carlisle

Junction
42

Golden
Fleece

A6

P ①

②

River
Petteril

③

Dalston

⑦

Newbiggin
Hall

Wreay
Woods

④

⑥

Low
Hurst

⑤

M6
South

WREAY

Wreay Hall
Mill

River Caldew

Start: White Bridge, Dalston **Grid ref:** NY371497   **Distance:** 6 miles/9.5 km
Maps: Landranger Sheet 85; Pathfinder 557 & 567 (NY34 & NY35)

Although the river looks peaceful most of the time, look for the effects of its power in the piles of logs and brash built up where it sweeps across its bends in flood, and in the expensive and futile attempts to keep it in its bed! The eastern bank has rough paths in places and is probably better completed while you are fresh. Boots or wellingtons essential: marshy in places. Parts of this side are still real 'countryside', with scrub, meadows, and wild flowers in abundance.

1 Start by the new White Bridge over the Caldew, and find footpath signs just east of the mill-leat. In season the woodlands are full of the four common warblers – in order of abundance, Willow, Blackcap, Chiffchaff, and Garden – and you will hear Whitethroat, Linnet and Yellowhammer in the gorse scrub. Common Sandpiper is unmissable throughout the summer, and you have a good chance of Kingfisher at any season. Goosander too is around all year.

2 Slumping and undercutting of the banks means you have to divert – follow the signs. Some sections are marshy; please avoid trampling marsh-plants by keeping on drier and firmer ground. In compensation for your trials there are Long-tailed Tit, Goldcrest and Treecreeper, and listen for the sharp *'chik'* calls of Great Spotted Woodpecker. Amongst the finches are Bullfinch, Goldfinch, Chaffinch and Greenfinch.

3 Pass under the railway about a hundred metres to the right of the river-bridge, then 200 metres further downstream cross the river itself at the footbridge. Dippers were feeding young here on my last visit, and there were two Kingfishers.

4 Back under the railway, Oystercatcher nests on the shingle beds, and Common Sandpiper, Grey and Pied Wagtail flutter ahead of you. In the alders look out for winter Redpoll and Siskin. A Great Grey Shrike spent a few winters in this area.

5 Beyond the weir, the right-of-way (and a new asphalt cycle-track) sticks to the side of the railway nearly back to Dalston. However, you can keep to the river-bank if you prefer. A series of fields below the sewage works presently act as settling beds, with pools and mud – check for waders. Although Redshank seems to have died out as a nesting species, Oystercatcher and Lapwing hang on.

6 The yellow waymarkers reappear to guide you through the new fences here, and back through a kissing-gate to the riverbank. Listen for Sedge Warbler in the overgrown willow-thickets approaching Dalston. Birds as varied as Night Heron and Red Kite have appeared in this part of the valley in recent times.

7 The path cuts back to the road between the schools. Walk through the village (stores, pubs) and you will see the White Bridge past the *cul-de-sac* signs.

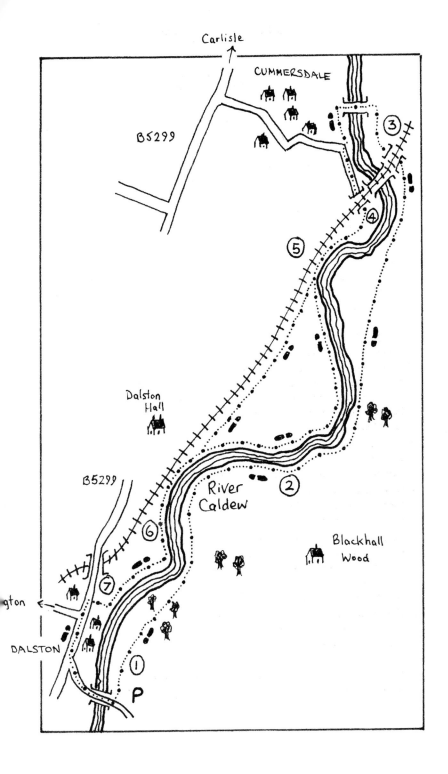

Carlisle

CUMMERSDALE

B5299

③

④

⑤

Dalston
Hall

B5299

River
Caldew

②

Blackhall
Wood

⑥

⑦

gton ←

DALSTON

①

P

Beckfoot & Allerdale Ramble

Start: Beckfoot   **Grid ref:** NY094497 **Distance:** 6 miles/9.5 km
Maps: Landranger Sheet 85; Pathfinder 556 (NY04, NY05, NY15)

Rather quiet in summer, but the open shore is packed with birds in other seasons. At low tide, the birds are far out on the tideline. For an hour or two on each side of the high tide, however, the waders and other birds are driven close enough to see them well from the edge of the dunes. At high tide the waders congregate on a few roosts, while the ducks and gulls often roost on the sea just offshore. The climate is rarely less than 'bracing', with onshore winds typical.

1 Park in any of the several gravel parks north and south of Beckfoot. A telescope (and firm tripod!) is a great bonus. Scaup and Red-breasted Merganser feed over the mussel beds at high tide, and when the mud is exposed, a great variety of waders feed. Watch the Herring Gulls trying to crack open mussels by dropping them on the shingle. Oystercatcher and Curlew are in big numbers, and Redshank and Ringed Plover should always be on view. Greenshank, Whimbrel, Grey Plover, Bar-tailed and Black-tailed Godwit all crop up from time to time. Further off-shore I have seen Harbour Porpoise and seals. In the dunes are Skylark, Meadow Pipit, and in winter Twite and Rock Pipit. A few years back, a Hoopoe survived the winter at Beckfoot, roosting in a garden, and feeding very successfully on chrysalises in the sand – so you can never predict what you might find!

2 Flocks of Golden Plover feed on the fields behind the dunes, and often come over to the shore to roost or to feed. Ruff sometimes joins them in passage seasons.

3 Check gorse areas for Stonechat at all seasons – there are a few nesting pairs – and Whitethroat and Linnet are common breeders. Sedge Warbler sings its chittering and grating song from ranker and damper ground, and Grasshopper Warbler is also possible: its reeling song is distinctive, but although the bird often sings from the top of a bush, it tends to remain hidden in a spray of leaves. At the far end of your walk, check the docks for gull species: Mediterranean Gull is on the list, and Silloth Docks are ripe for a really rare gull! Flocks of Redshank sometimes roost over the high tide on the superstructures. The esplanade north from the docks is also worth checking in winter: close views of Turnstone flocks are likely, with other waders such as those mentioned above.

4 Back along the footpaths you should see abundant Greenfinch and Goldfinch, Collared Dove, etc. In spring, keep an eye on any pairs of Shelduck flighting over the golfcourse and nearby fields: they may be prospecting for a nest site, perhaps down a rabbit-hole, and you may see the pair swoop low, and one of the birds drop to the ground, suddenly to disappear down a hole you hadn't seen!

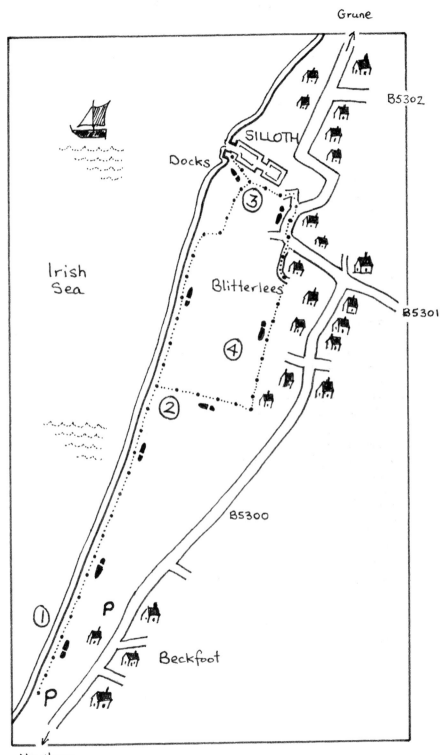

Grune

B5302

SILLOTH

Docks

③

Irish
Sea

Blitterlees

④

B5301

②

B5300

①

P

P

Beckfoot

Grune Point & Solway Firth

Start: Silloth shore road **Grid ref:** NY114548 **Distance:** 4½ miles/7 km
Maps: Landranger Sheet 85; Pathfinder 556 (NY15)

Good at any time of year, with the best variety in migration seasons. This area is not very thoroughly covered: in the right conditions it can turn up some real rarities!

Waders and waterfowl are best observed around high water, when roosting waders are pushed up onto the marsh just across the creek from Grune. Spring tides are best.

If parking, use any of the several car-parks or lay-bys north from Silloth. The shorter the walk you want, the nearer Skinburness you park!

1 The promenade can be very exposed in westerlies, but this is when you stand the best chance of Storm and Leach's Petrels, skuas, and other birds which usually stay far from shore. In calm conditions there are Turnstone and other waders, and flocks of Scaup sometimes ride very close in to the groynes. The sea is usually quiet, but if the tides are running, flocks of Bar-tailed Godwit and Knot rush by a little off-shore.

2 Keep to the shore here and follow the 'Cumbria Coastal Way' signs. Terns of several species may be passing or feeding close by, and keep an eye open for Mediterranean Gull: one wintered on this stretch from Silloth to Grune for many years. Up to three thousand Knot roost on Skinburnessbank at times.

3 The great swathes of gorse have Linnet and Whitethroat in summer, and Willow Warbler wherever there are taller hawthorns. Check carefully all the grassy areas between the gorse, along the hedges and in the fields which run down the ridge of Grune Point itself. Spring migrants include Wheatear and warblers; Skylark and Meadow Pipit breed; and in autumn look for Redstart, Goldcrest, and often migrating Blue and Coal Tit. Winter has Reed Bunting in the gorse and the marram, and there are always surprises – a Shorelark wintered at the tip of the point for two seasons, and Hoopoe was present in autumn 2000.

4 Please respect the signs which you may see in summer intended to reduce disturbance to nesting birds: keep to the path. Oystercatcher is especially noticeable, but Ringed Plover is much more circumspect!

5 Scan in all directions. Best are calm days and rising tides, when Scaup in flocks come up the bay and into the creeks. Red-breasted Merganser, Great Crested Grebe and divers (usually Red-throated, but Black-throated and Great Northern also at times) are often seen. Waders – sometimes in great numbers – come to roost on the saltmarsh across the main creek to the south. Oystercatcher is in spectacular thousands, often with Grey Plover, Curlew, Bar-tailed Godwit, Redshank and Knot. The smaller waders are mostly Dunlin, with an admixture of Ringed Plover and Sanderling. Black-tailed Godwit, Whimbrel, Greenshank and Spotted Redshank all occur with some regularity; the last two have over-wintered. Cormorant nests on the distant pilings, Shelduck is abundant at all seasons, Golden Plover winters on the marsh. Watch for sudden flushes of the birds: Peregrine, Merlin or Sparrowhawk are often the cause. Recent rarities have included Black-winged Pratincole and Pacific Golden Plover.

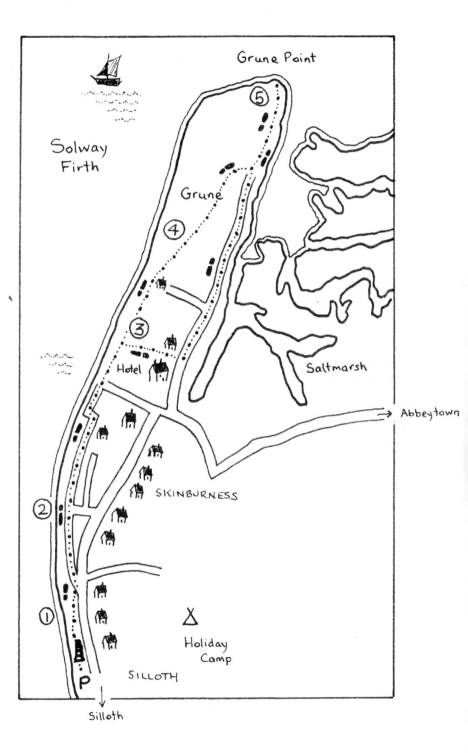

Grune Point

Solway
Firth

⑤

Grune

④

③

Hotel

Saltmarsh

Abbeytown

②

SKINBURNESS

①

✕
Holiday
Camp

SILLOTH

P

Silloth

Bowness-on-Solway & Campfield Marsh

Start: Bowness Railings   **Grid ref:** NY232627   **Distance:** 5 miles/8 km
Maps: Landranger Sheet 85; Pathfinder 543 & 544 (NY16 & NY26)

Beware of the highest tides: the road is covered by higher spring tides at several places (marked by warning signs). Port Carlisle and right round to Cardurnock and Anthorn can all be good, the main problem being the viewing distance. Telescope an advantage! Rarities seen along this coast in recent years include Long-billed Dowitcher, American Wigeon, Pacific and American Golden Plovers and Spoonbill.

Park at any of the places marked on the map; if parking elsewhere, be very careful to avoid obstructing the narrow road. A car, however, often makes a good hide, or a shelter from the often severe winds. Sites are dealt with from east to west.

1 'Bowness railings': a pull-off by the seat on the promontory. At high tide, waders may be pushed up close to the railings. You may get close views of smaller waders (especially Ringed Plover and Dunlin), but they are easily flushed by an incautious approach. Little Stint and Curlew Sandpiper are here in 'good' autumns for these. Waders such as Redshank and Golden Plover roost to the east on the grass. Watch for Great Crested Grebe, divers, Red-breasted Merganser and Scaup on the rising tide.

2 'The Shelter': Follow footpath signs in the village to 'The Banks'. This provides some shelter in bad weather. Possibility of passage birds as 1 above and 3 below.

3 'The Viaduct': This is not a public right of way, and we cannot therefore advise you to walk it. That said, this is *the* place to watch for passage of skuas in April/May. Pomarine Skua is the main species sought; all four species are possible. Very unpredictable! Kittiwakes, Fulmars, terns, ducks and auks also possible. Don't expect close views! These can of course be seen from points 1, 2 or 4, but even more distant.

4 Campfield Marsh: RSPB-managed saltmarsh, with big roosts of waders at high tide; two 'dedicated' laybys (here and at 7). Look especially for Grey and Golden Plover, Knot, Bar-tailed and Black-tailed Godwits, among the many Curlew and Oyster-catcher. Mallard, Wigeon and Shelduck are frequent, Pintail, Teal and Shoveler less so. When the birds all flush, look for the source: Sparrowhawk, Merlin or Peregrine. Short-eared and Barn Owl possible.

5 Bowness Gravel Pits Cumbria Wildlife Trust Reserve: A pretty reliable site for Willow Tit at any season (listen for distinctive low *'bzz ... bzz ... bzz ... bzz'* call-notes); nesting Whitethroat, Sedge Warbler, Blackcap, and other warblers.

6 Several pools behind screened banks courtesy of RSPB. Excellent close views of nesting Lapwing in summer, with Little Grebe, Redshank, Oystercatcher, Curlew, Black-headed Gull, Shelduck, Shoveler, Wigeon, Teal amongst other likely sightings.

7 The layby here overlooks a pool and the largest high-tide roost, best at spring tides when the birds are pushed closest. Waders, Shelduck, and other ducks. Do not walk out on to the marsh: the birds badly need the secure roost-site in harsh winter weather.

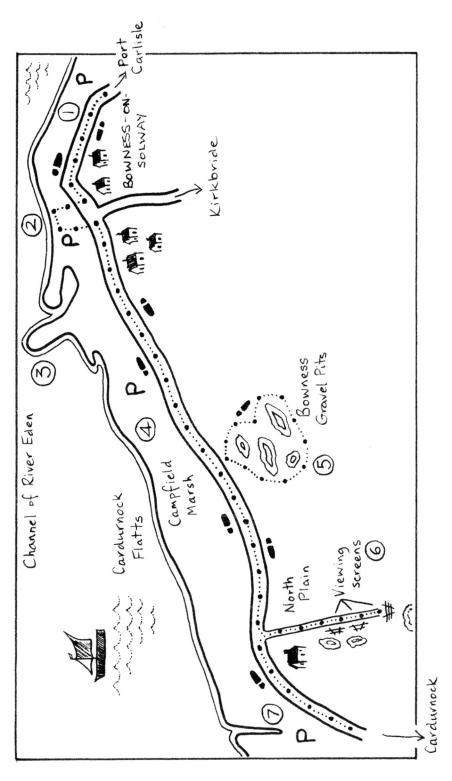

Channel of River Eden

Cardurnock Flatts

Campfield Marsh

Bowness Gravel Pits

North Plain

Viewing Screens

BOWNESS-ON-SOLWAY

Port Carlisle

Kirkbride

Cardurnock

① P
② P
③
④ P
⑤
⑥
⑦ P

Burgh Marsh

Start: Boustead Hill   **Grid ref:** NY294594   **Distance:** 7½ miles/12 km
Maps: Landranger Sheet 85; Pathfinder 554 & 557 (NY25, 35 & NY36)

Prime saltmarsh in National Trust care; interesting birds throughout the year. Do not go out when spring tides are running: the whole marsh can be flooded! Always follow a falling tide. Plank bridges cross the main creeks, but if you happen to miss these, prepare to get very muddy. Very exposed to the north: be prepared. It is often much colder out on the point than where you started! The main loop walk is long; the OS map marks shorter escape routes. Keep to paths, and leash dogs: nesting waders.

This area is still little covered by the bird-watchers; it would undoubtedly turn up many more good birds than are ever reported. Keep your eyes peeled at all times; the open expanses attract migrants from afar.

1 Head straight out. In late winter, there may be many geese, especially Barnacle. Shelduck will be feeding in pools, and in spring flying over, whistling, to prospect nest-holes under the gorse. The short turf has Lapwing and Skylark in summer, and a few Redshank and Curlew make a noisy presence where the marsh is more tussocky and rushy. Snipe and Grey Heron feed in creeks and wet hollows, and there are a surprising number of pools out there – Wheatear, Green Sandpiper and Greenshank in spring and late summer migration, Teal and Wigeon in winter, off-duty Redshank in summer.

2 At the estuary-edge, turn right and follow the (faint) track eastwards. Cormorant and various sort of ducks, waders and gulls feed and roost in the estuary. One April morning, I found a Dotterel pottering along the edge. The tip of Rockcliffe Marsh to the north has a huge colony of gulls, and through April Barnacle Geese bathe in the runnels, and feed up on the 'spring bite' in preparation for their return to Arctic Svalbard. Unfortunately fighter-pilots enjoy beating up the estuary; at least you then get to see just how many geese there *are*, as they flush! Pink-footed Geese and rarely other species also often accompany the Barnacles.

3 The 'basin' at low tide gathers great numbers of waders, gulls and ducks: Golden Plover and more rarely Ruff mix with the Lapwing flocks; in winter look out for all three 'sawbill' ducks – Smew, Goosander and Red-breasted Merganser. Look for rare waders. A Whooper Swan herd is regular. If everything to the horizon flies up in a panic, expect a Peregrine. Smaller 'panics' may mean Merlin or Sparrowhawk.

4 The tidal reaches of the Eden. Many Goldeneye winter; the drakes' wings whistle as they whizz by. Huge numbers of gulls flight back and forth to feeding grounds inland, and Curlew and Lapwing also make regular roosting flights down-river at dusk.

5 Walk back through Holmesmill and up the lane towards Burgh-by-Sands through fields which in winter sometimes hold Pink-footed Goose, and more usually Fieldfare and Redwing. Grey Partridge make their scratchy calls in spring.

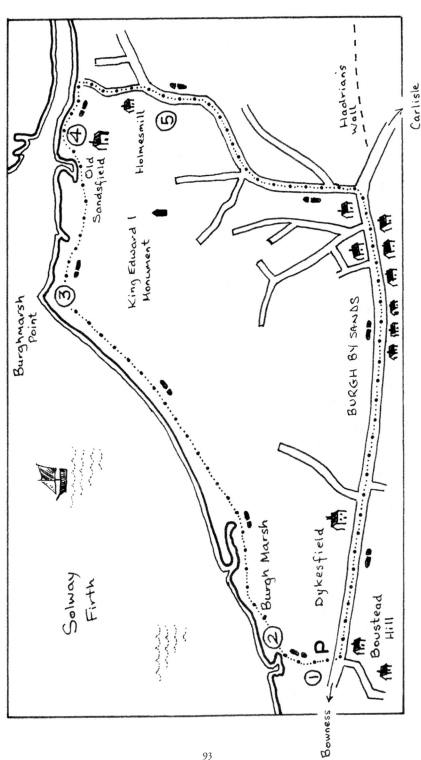

Solway Firth

Burghmarsh Point

Burgh Marsh

Old Sandsfield

Holmesmill

King Edward I Monument

BURGH BY SANDS

Dykesfield

Boustead Hill

Hadrian's Wall

Carlisle

Bowness

P

① ② ③ ④ ⑤

Carlisle Swifts & River Eden

Start: see below   **Grid ref:** NY394566   **Distance:** you choose!
(Caldew Bridge)
Maps: Landranger Sheet 85; Pathfinder 557 & 558 (NY35 & NY45)

A delightful walk – one of the nicest in the local area, in spite of the general human bustle – with easy access from the city, and variety of easy-to-see species. Choose your own route. Walk down from the town, past the castle, or through the Sands Centre or the golf course; or park in Rickerby Park and walk from there. You will see many other paths on the maps: lengthen or shorten at will.

All on good paths. Plenty of birds all year, but best in late spring/early summer. All paths get busier (with humans!) at weekends.

Otter has recently been seen, even at mid-day! Look for tracks and 'spraints'.

1 Look from the bridge for Kingfisher and Grey Wagtail; Dipper at least in winter. Song Thrushes are notably abundant. Sparrowhawk probably nests nearby. In winter watch at the confluence of the Caldew and Eden for Tufted Duck, Goldeneye, and Goosander. Goosander can usually be seen with ducklings in June/July, and many more Mallard broods; even Red-breasted Merganser has bred.

2 The superb riverside stands of tall herbs and sallows are crowded with Sedge Warblers in season: I have never seen anywhere such a density of this bird as here in 1997! Also many other warblers: Willow and Garden, Chiffchaff, Blackcap, Whitethroat. Wren, Goldfinch, Linnet, Redpoll are in the weeds, and Moorhen, Mallard, Common Sandpiper and Grey Heron are present. With luck, a pair of Reed Bunting. Kingfisher certainly nests, and try to count the Sand Martin holes all the way along: in great numbers in recent years, having recovered their numbers spectacularly after their population crash a decade ago. In June look out for the very rare, but here abundant, Warty Cabbage: tall spikes of yellow flowers, and curious globular fruits.

3 Coming out from the golf course, the meadows here are (presently) undeveloped and unspoiled: listen for Skylark, and watch for Oystercatcher. Mute Swan sometimes nests along this stretch. Little Grebe winters, but can be very inconspicuous! Sand Martin is again abundant, and often joined by feeding Swift, House Martin and Swallow, especially in the passage seasons.

4 If you can bear the racket from the motorway, follow the river up to the bends beyond it. This area has produced many good birds such as Whiskered Tern, Mediterranean Gull, Black-tailed Godwit and many other species of migrant waders. In winter, Smew are sometimes present, along with a flock of hundreds of Wigeon, and variable numbers of Greylag and Pink-footed Geese and Whooper Swan. Merlin, Buzzard, Sparrowhawk and Peregrine can all be seen. The last three of these are also possible in summer. Osprey is appearing more often. Oystercatcher, Ringed Plover, Curlew and Lapwing nest. That beautiful damselfly, the Banded Demoiselle, seems to have successfully recolonised the river.

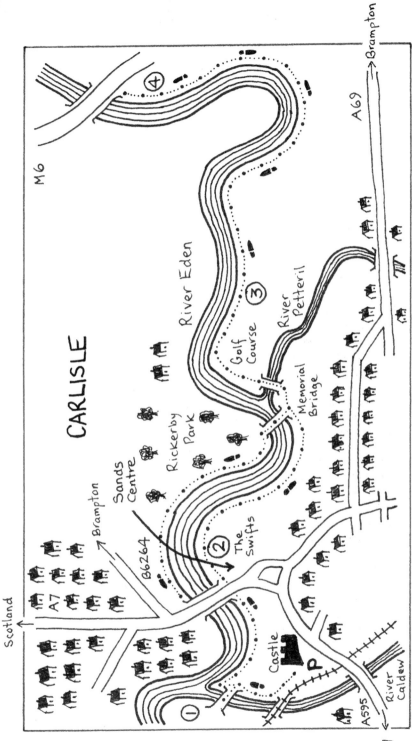

CARLISLE

M6

River Eden

Scotland

A7

B6264

Brampton

Sands Centre

Rickerby Park

The Swifts

Golf Course

Memorial Bridge

River Petteril

A69 → Brampton

Castle

P

A595

River Caldew

Thursby

① ② ③ ④

95

River Eden Gorge

Start: Wetheral village green **Grid ref:** NY466544 **Distance:** 9½ miles/15 km
Maps: Landranger Sheet 85; Pathfinder 558 & 568 (NY44, 45 & NY54)

The spectacular Eden gorge, part of which is explored on this walk, was carved after the Ice Age when melt-waters were blocked by a 'stagnant' glacier from their normal course (down the valley of the 'now-Petteril'). There are few points of public access to the river-side path between Wetheral Woods and Froddle Crook, and the walk on rights-of-way and back along the road is long. With a lift or public transport, you might save the walk back, or turn round and come back from whatever point you reach in the valley – as I generally do. Certainly one tends to see several fresh species for the day while returning along the same track!

1 From the village green walk down past the historic old church of the Holy Trinity. At the river look for Dipper, Goosander, and Grey Wagtail (all three occur throughout this river-walk), and Kestrel by the famous viaduct, then turn right (upstream), and follow the path opposite Corby Castle with its Jackdaw colony and rookery. Stock Doves are here, but in lesser numbers than Woodpigeons.

2 The path goes up some stone steps opposite the 'waterfall' (which only runs when pumped!), then along into Wetheral Woods (National Trust). Chiffchaff, Garden Warbler and Blackcap are all common in summer, and Great Spotted Woodpecker, Treecreeper and Goldcrest are year-round residents. Long-tailed Tit is usually the commonest tit, but Great, Blue, Coal, and a pair or two of Marsh Tit are all here. Nuthatch has established a presence in recent years. Follow a lower path to 'St Constantine's Cells', and a fine view over the river. Several Spotted Flycatcher and sometimes Pied Flycatcher summer hereabouts.

3 Follow signs for 'Footpath in Eden Valley' past Cote House and Brackenbank. NB: sections of this path are presently muddy and overgrown. Buzzard and Sparrowhawk are frequent, and Peregrine also hunts along the valley at times. Little Grebe and Goldeneye winter, with numbers of Greylag Goose and Tufted Duck, which also now nest (look for the tight groups of ducklings very late in the summer). Osprey is appearing more often, and will colonise, given the chance.

4 Opposite the cottage in Fishgarth Wood, a wooden sign indicates the steep path up to Froddle Crook on the main road, or the river path continues up past more delightful scenery to Low House, where again you can regain the road. There are fine views across to the Lake District hills, and in winter you may see Greylag Geese and many Fieldfare and Redwing. Common Gull is an abundant winterer too, and in late afternoon, huge numbers flight over on their way back to the Solway to roost.

5 At Wetheral Shield, a path is signed back to Wetheral, but can be difficult to follow over the fields. Otherwise keep to the road. Tree Sparrows and Yellowhammers are still to be seen, and Sedge Warbler and Whitethroat nest where the hedges are thicker, or have nettle beds alongside. Grasshopper Warbler can sometimes be heard singing in calm dusks from the pools on the west of the road at Cotehill, and Buzzard nests in the tall trees in the hedges.

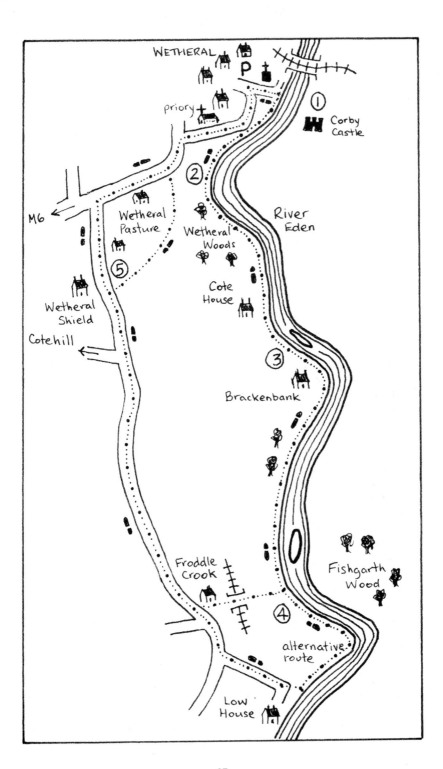

Upper Geltsdale

Start: Jockey Shield **Grid ref:** NY557556 **Distance:** 5 miles/8 km

(7 miles/11 km)

Maps: Landranger Sheet 85; Pathfinder 558 (NY55)

Although this landscape is completely created by man over a very long period of time, with its mining, deforestation, re-afforestation, stock-grazing, and moor-burning, nonetheless it has a fine wild character, and is popular with local walkers for that reason. In winter it is barren and windswept in the extreme, and Carrion Crow and Red Grouse may be the only birds you see up on the moors, with not many more in the valley. In summer the moors come alive with birds, and there are many species upon which to test out your skills and patience. Two walks are described. Parts are managed by RSPB: more sensitive management techniques are already bearing fruit.

From Jockey Shield drop down to the River Gelt bridge. Follow the track left up through the birches, and join the rough 'road' at the wooden gate. (Also a pleasant walk to this spot from Talkin village, via Talkin Head.) In spring, Mistle Thrush and Yellowhammer, and in winter, Fieldfare and Redwing instead.

1 Go right, up the track, out on to the open moor (past well-named 'The Greens' cottage – the thick green turf here indicates the limestone outcropping below) and then on to the old shooting lodge of 'Gairs'.

2 Red Grouse should soon make their presence known at least by their crowing calls up on the heather, and there are Curlew and Lapwing on the rushy flat shoulders below. Black Grouse, bucking the national trend of long-term decline, have appeared in recent years: watch out for them on the lower flanks, perhaps incongruously perched up in spindly birches and hawthorns along the tracks. The cocks' astonishing bubbling display can be heard in calm dusks, when Woodcock may 'rode' overhead, Snipe may 'drum' and Long-eared, Barn, and Tawny Owls set off to hunt. Meadow Pipit and Skylark are abundant; Ring Ouzel much rarer, and on the higher slopes only. Golden Plover may also come song-flighting over from the high moors.

3 From just beyond Gairs a rather faint path drops down the south side of How Gill and back to the road below Geltsdale House. Tree Pipit, Redstart and Pied Flycatcher occur in the stream-side trees and on the wooded slopes.

4 However, for a splendid longer walk (7 miles/11 km), follow the track south below Tarnmonath Fell, down to Old Water Bridge, and down the Old Water beck to Binneybank (5), where you pick up the road back. All along the upland stretch of this route, at least in summer, watch out for Peregrine, Hen Harrier, Merlin, Short-eared Owl, Buzzard and Raven, any of which might sail into view over the crest of the hill, or be quartering the moors. Your best chances are to sit on a clear day and scan patiently with binoculars. Often the large bird soaring majestically in the distance reveals itself as it approaches to be merely a Curlew in display! These birds are characteristic of heather moors. If you fail to spot them in this place, ponder that there have been recent cases of poisoning, nest-destruction and shooting of birds of prey – all totally illegal acts – in this grouse-shooters' domain.

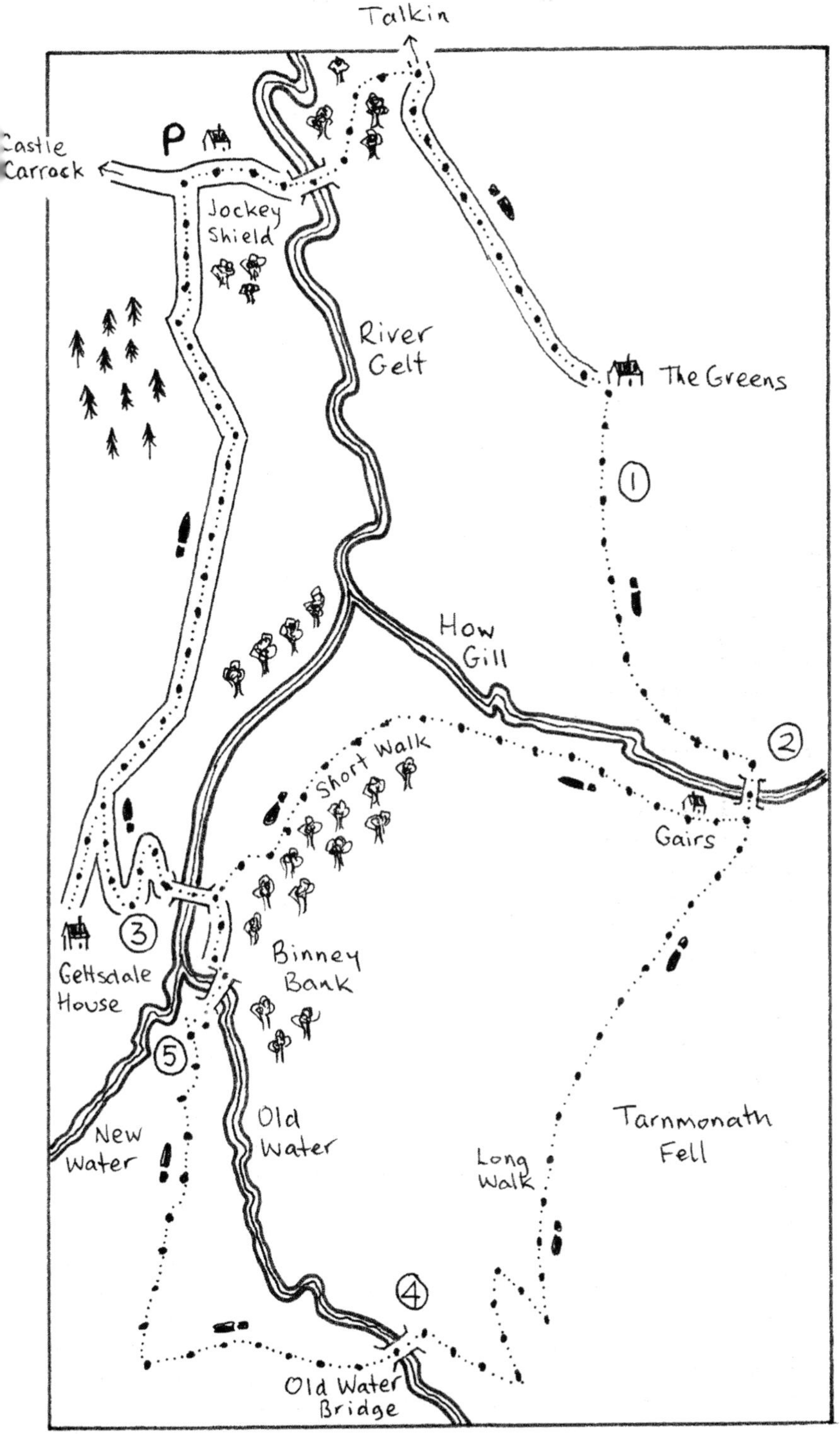

Talkin

Castle
Carrock ←

P

Jockey
Shield

River
Gelt

The Greens

①

How
Gill

②

Short Walk

Gairs

③

Geltsdale
House

Binney
Bank

⑤

New
Water

Old
Water

Tarnmonath
Fell

Long
Walk

④

Old Water
Bridge

Middle Gelt Woods

Start: Lower Gelt Bridge   **Grid ref:** NY520592   **Distance:** 3½ miles/5.5 km
Maps: Landranger Sheet 86; Pathfinder 558 (NY55)

A pleasant walk through woods, alongside the River Gelt. The paths are mostly good, though a little muddy in places. Better variety of birds in summer.

Turn off the A69 at the sign for 'Hayton Town Head', after 250m turn left over the river, and park in the little car-park immediately on the right. The paths run through oak and beech woods for 2 km, at times close to the river, and at other times far above it. In season, there are Pied Flycatchers (nesting in the many boxes scattered through the woods), Wood Warbler on the steep slopes (they nest in low cover below the oak trees), Garden Warbler, and the expected Willow Warbler, Jay, Coal, Long-tailed, and other tits, Treecreeper, etc. One year a Sparrowhawk nested in a tangle of ivy below the path, so that you could look down upon the incubating female. Listen out for Nuthatches, which are in the process of colonising northeast Cumbria.

1 Beyond the little bridge over the Hell Beck, there may be Marsh Tit in the young birches, and Chiffchaff in the dense mixed plantations, and perhaps more pairs of Wood Warbler. Dipper can be seen singing along the stream for most of the year.

2 At Middle Gelt Bridge, below the fine railway viaduct on the Newcastle line, look for Grey Wagtail upstream of the bridge. Kestrel nests in the top end of the wood.

3 Turn right and up the hill, and just over the crest of the hill, opposite 'Tow Top', follow the footpath sign to the right. Take the waymarked and stiled path for 2 km NNW through plantations and fields back to the start. Listen for the loud 'chick' call of Great Spotted Woodpecker in the mature woods. In the open country Linnet still nests in the remaining gorse patches.

Whilst you are in the area, there are two good bird walks to explore close at hand. Both are accessible from the B6413 south from Brampton. Talkin Tarn is well sign-posted from the A69. It is now a 'country park', and very full of visitors and boats in summer especially. In spite of the people pressure, it can be very rewarding at all times of the year. In summer, Pied Flycatcher is frequent, and can be easily observed feeding young in the nestboxes. In winter, a large gull roost collects in the late afternoon, and there are always Pochard, Tufted Duck, Goldeneye, Mallard, and often rarer waterfowl. Recent years have seen Red-throated Diver, Red-necked Grebe, Smew, Long-tailed and Ring-necked Duck on the tarn, and – in good beech-mast seasons – up to a thousand Bramblings.

Castle Carrock reservoir lies just south of the village of the same name, and a path leads right round it. It is best in winter, with often large numbers of ducks such as Mallard, Teal, Wigeon, Pochard, Tufted Duck and Goldeneye, and you may see Greylag Goose, and Great Crested and Little Grebe.

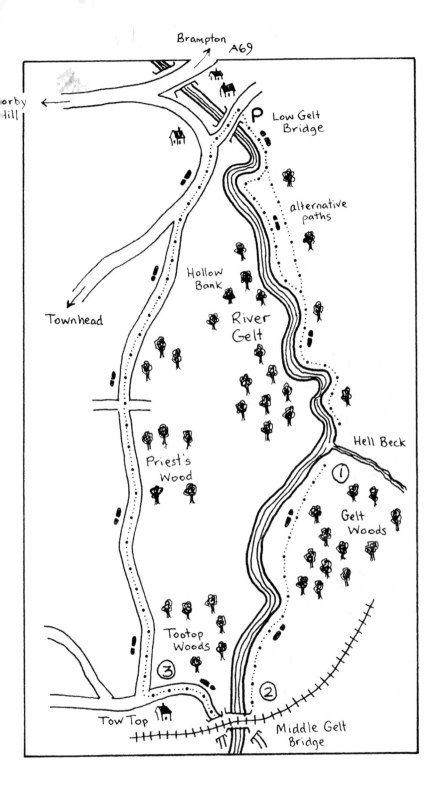

Brampton A69

orby
Hill

Low Gelt
Bridge

P

alternative
paths

Townhead

Hollow
Bank

River
Gelt

Hell Beck

Priest's
Wood

①

Gelt
Woods

②

Tootop
Woods

③

Tow Top

Middle Gelt
Bridge

Longtown Ponds & River Esk

Start: Longtown   **Grid ref:** NY379687   **Distance:** 9 miles/14.5 km
Maps: Landranger Sheet 85; Pathfinder 531 & 544 (NY36 & NY37)

Longtown is at the centre of a selection of gravel pits, and the Esk attracts many birds at all times of the year. This walk looks at some of the best areas. Park in Longtown on the street. There are several possibilities to pursue, depending on time.

1   Walk down Esk Street, continuing along the river bank to where you can overlook the Arthuret ponds. Good all year. Great Crested Grebe, Little Grebe, Sedge Warbler, and many other waterfowl and other birds in summer; Goosander, and with luck Green Sandpiper, Short-eared Owl or Smew in winter.

2   Cross Esk Bridge and overlook the two pools on the south of the road. Try to ignore the incessant traffic-noise! A very good variety of waterfowl is usually visible here, with Shoveler and Cormorant regular, a good flock of wintering Wigeon, Teal roosting in numbers under the sallows, and many diving ducks. Tufted Duck, Goldeneye and Pochard are regular, and other rarer visitors have included the elusive Smew (often), Long-tailed and Ferruginous Ducks, the rarer grebes and occasional divers. The alder/willow copses to the southeast of Smalmstown Terrace often have Willow Tit, and in winter Siskin and Redpoll.

3   Follow the footpath sign just west of the bridge round the back of the factory and cut across to the river bank. The stretch upstream for a kilometre has a record of attracting good birds in season. Little Gull, and at times Black Tern, occurs in some years in the period late April to early June. Common Tern penetrates this far up-river to feed. Goosander, Red-breasted Merganser, Shelduck, Ringed Plover, Redshank, Common Sandpiper, and Oystercatcher all breed, and you should see Yellow, Pied and Grey Wagtail, and perhaps Kingfisher. In passage seasons there have been Wood Sandpiper, Black-tailed Godwit, Little Ringed Plover and Osprey, and rarer birds have included Spotted Sandpiper. There are several delightful Sand Martin colonies.

4   Return by the same route to Longtown, or if you want to enlarge the day-list with a longer walk, cross the A7 at NY380711, and continue up past Batenbush, turning left after a wood on the left. At the end of the lane (5), follow the bridle-path sign for 'Beckside' into the woods. Follow the track curving to the left after 150m, and follow this rutted track until you meet a larger east-west ride. Turn left for Beckside. In the lower birch and hazel scrub, listen for abundant Garden Warbler, and in the high mixed wood beyond, Blackcap, and the usual Treecreeper, Goldcrest etc. You should see Buzzard, and perhaps hear Wood Warbler and Pied Flycatcher. At Beckside, walk back to the A7, past Oakbank pools (6). You can pay at the office to walk round here, and view the ponds – well worth it. Great Crested and Little Grebes in summer, Whooper Swans winter here or on the fields with various geese, and watch for Smew amongst the many ducks. Walk back to Longtown on the A7, partly on pavement.

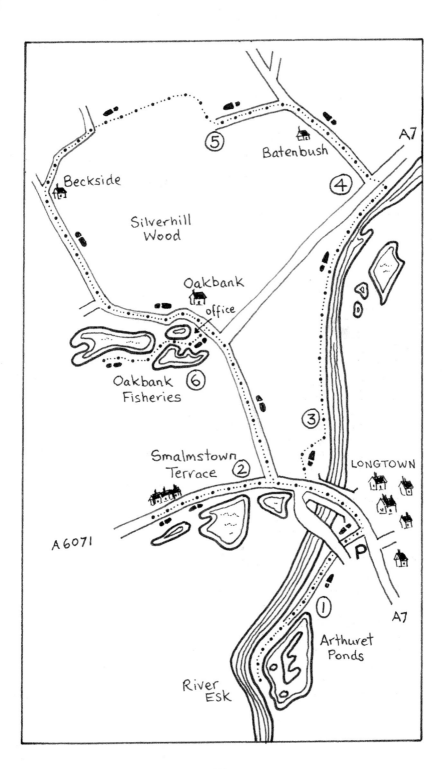

A7

⑤

Batenbush

④

Beckside

Silverhill
Wood

Oakbank
🏠 office

⑥

Oakbank
Fisheries

D

③

Smalmstown
Terrace ②

LONGTOWN

A6071

P

①

A7

Arthuret
Ponds

River
Esk

Tindale Tarn

Start: Tindale village   **Grid ref:** NY617593   **Distance:** 4½ miles/7.5 km
Maps: Landranger Sheet 86; Pathfinder 558 & 559 (NY55 & NY65)

Tindale Tarn, with its north exposure and altitude (215 metres, 700 feet), is – as you may judge – exposed and wild, although with the woods and farm overlooking it, it can be pleasant enough in summer. At times, after a good growth of pondweed, there are impressive winter flocks of ducks and swans.

1 Turn off the A689 at the sign for Tindale, and park on waste ground next to the low trees. Drop down to the bridge, checking for Pied and Grey Wagtail, and then right over a stile and follow yellow waymarkers past old workings and limekilns with Wheatear. Curlew, Skylark and Meadow Pipit will be singing over the slopes in spring. At the tin shacks go through the gate, past a sign presently saying "Private – No fishing – RSPB". Listen for singing Redshank in the marshy fields.

2 Walk through the farmyard of Tarn House, closing all gates after you. Willow Warbler, Spotted Flycatcher, Redstart and Goldfinch should be about the farm and woods in summer. The tarn may be scanned from several points along this track. Where the waterbirds collect depends on wind, weather and species. Great Crested Grebe, Mallard, Tufted Duck, Mute Swan and Teal are likely in summer, and in winter, perhaps a greater variety with many Coot, Wigeon, Pochard, Canada Geese, Whooper Swan, and other species. Red-crested Pochard is among the rare visitors worth checking for. In the reed and sedge fringes of the tarn in summer will be Sedge Warbler and Reed Bunting. Reed Warbler has been recorded.

3 For a quick return (3 miles/5km) stay on the track as it curves across the valley up to 'Thorn', and back to Tindale. Or go straight ahead at the wooden gate, following the yellow waymarkers. The limestone outcrops above you also have Wheatear – with noisy chacking family parties by early June – and Meadow Pipit. Cuckoo and Whinchat may be seen along this section.

4 Lapwing is declining even here in the rough grassland, but if present will dive-bomb you rather disconcertingly when defending chicks. Look for Kestrel over the fell-sides. At 'Howgill' go through the gate and turn right into the lane. Linnet inhabits the old mine-workings to the left. Rushy hollows have Curlew and a few Redshank and Snipe, and you should hear Reed Bunting again. Any Pipits perching in the young trees in the plantation here will be Meadow and not Tree Pipits!

5 Turn right at the sign for 'Tindale via Tarn'. Don't miss the fine vista to the north over the border forests. At Thorn follow the waymarkers out onto the open fell through the wicket gate. The path contours along the top of the fell. Curlew – along with Lapwing – have been abundant here in the past, with some Redshank, but seem to be suffering under the present widespread 'intensification' of agriculture.

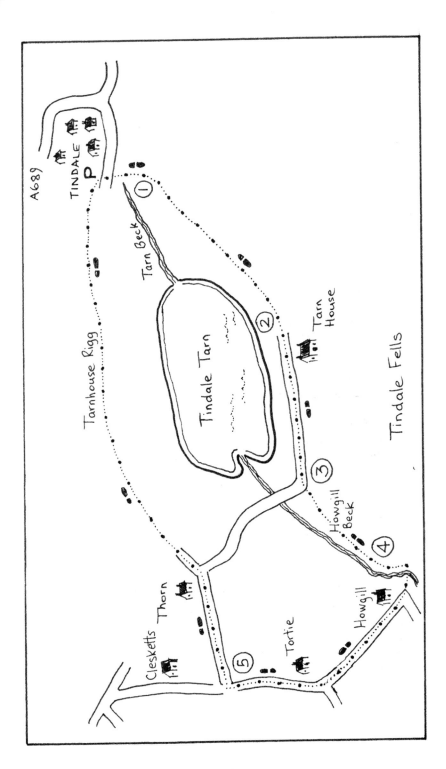

A689

TiNDALE

P

Tarn Beck

Tarnhouse Rigg

①

Tindale Tarn

②

Tarn House

③

Howgill Beck

④

Tindale Fells

Clesketts Thorn

⑤

Tortie

Howgill

Transport

Some of our walks start from fairly remote points. If you are reliant upon public transport to reach the start points, the following information may help.

The essential booklet is the free *Getting around Cumbria and the Lake District*, which is published twice a year by Cumbria County Council. This includes huge amounts of information for residents and visitors, including rail services to or within Cumbria (including steam railways), boat services and buses. This may be obtained from any of the Tourist Information Centres below, or from Cumbria County Council Public Transport Team, Citadel Chambers, Carlisle CA3 8SG.

Stagecoach Cumberland has a brochure of bus times and route maps, also available from Tourist Information Centres.

Telephone Helpline
There is a telephone helpline on 0870 608 2 608, available from 7 a.m. to 9 p.m. seven days a week, for all public transport enquiries.

On the Internet
The 'Cumbria Journey Planner' public transport information system is on the internet and now includes all national train times. This system allows you to select where in Cumbria you wish to travel, then in seconds will give you all the bus, train and lake steamer times you need. The site is at http://www.cumbria.gov-uk. Journey Planner on CD-Rom is also available from Cumbria County Council for a small charge.

Tourist Information Centres

Alston, Town Hall	01434 381696
Ambleside, Market Cross	015394 32582
Appleby-in-Westmorland, Moot Hall	017683 51177
Barrow-in-Furness, Forum 28, Duke Street	01229 894784
Bowness-on-Windermere, Glebe Road	015394 42895
Brampton, Moot Hall	016977 3433
Broughton-in-Furness, The Square	01229 716115
Carlisle, Old Town Hall	01228 625600
Cockermouth, Town Hall	09100 822634
Coniston, Main Car Park	015394 41533
Cumbrian Gateway, M6 Lancaster Services	01524 792181

Egremont, Main Street	01946 820693
Grange-over-Sands, Main Street	015395 34026
Grasmere, Red Bank Road	015394 35245
Hawkshead, Main Car Park	015394 36525
Kendal, Town Hall	01539 725758
Keswick, Moot Hall	017687 72645
Killington Lake, M6 Southbound	015396 20138
Kirkby Lonsdale, Main Street	015242 71437
Kirkby Stephen, Market Square	017683 71199
Longtown, Community Centre	01228 792835
Maryport, Maritime Museum	01900 813738
Penrith, Museum	01768 867466
Pooley Bridge, The Square	017684 86530
Seatoller, Borrowdale	017684 77294
Sedbergh, Main Street	015396 20125
Sellafield, Visitors Centre	019467 76510
Silloth-on-Solway, The Green	016973 31944
Southwaite, M6 Services	016974 73445
Ullswater, Glenridding	017684 82414
Ulverston, Coronation Hall	01229 587120
Waterhead, Ambleside	015394 32729
Whitehaven, Market Hall	01946 852939
Windermere, Victoria Street	015394 46499
Workington, Carnegie Theatre	01900 60669

Seasonal Occurrence Chart

There are as many variations in the seasonal occurrence of birds in Cumbria as there are species listed below. Decisions on how to categorise each bird's occurrence have therefore been to an extent subjective.

The abundances are those of the bird within its range in the county. Thus Nuthatch is common and likely to be recorded within its limited range in the south of the county, but is much more scattered in the north and west of the county. For the Cumbrian range, see the *Atlas of Breeding Birds of Britain and Ireland* and the forthcoming *Atlas of Breeding Birds in Cumbria*.

Whether the species is encountered will depend upon the experience of the observer: knowing where to look, familiarity with calls/songs etc.

Bear in mind that the chart masks large movements between habitats, so that, for example, Meadow Pipit is common in the fell-country in summer, but largely abandons this habitat in winter, when it becomes common in lowland fields, marshes, etc.; Twite is rare in summer, largely in the hills, and much more frequent in winter, but in a different habitat, i.e. saltmarsh and coastal fields.

Birds are listed in the chart in alphabetical order of common name.

▮ frequent and likely to be encountered in appropriate habitat and within its range in the county.

▮ present in small numbers, and might be encountered in appropriate habitat and within its range in the county.

▮ a few present: unlikely to be encountered.

No indication: only very exceptional presence: if you think you have seen a bird not in the chart, have you identified it correctly?

The following birds are mentioned in the walk texts, but are only occasional visitors, or if regular or resident are extremely rare; they are not listed in the chart:

American Golden Plover; American Wigeon; Avocet; Bearded Tit; Bittern; Caspian Tern; Black-winged Pratincole; Crane; Ferruginous Duck; Golden Eagle; Golden Oriole; Great Grey Shrike; Grey Phalarope; Hooded Crow; Hoopoe; Long-billed Dowitcher; Long-tailed Duck; Muscovy Duck; Night Heron; Pacific Golden Plover; Pectoral Sandpiper; Red Kite; Red-crested Pochard; Red-necked Grebe; Ring-necked Duck; Ross's Gull; Rough-legged Buzzard; Shore Lark; Snow Goose; Spoonbill; Spotted Sandpiper; Whiskered Tern; Yellow-legged Gull.

	Jan	Feb	Mar	Apr	May	Jun	Jul	Aug	Sept	Oct	Nov	Dec
Arctic Skua												
Arctic Tern												
Bar-headed Goose												
Bar-tailed Godwit												
Barn Owl												
Barnacle Goose												
Black Grouse												
Black Guillemot												
Black Redstart												
Black Tern												
Black-headed Gull												
Black-necked Grebe												
Black-tailed Godwit												
Black-throated Diver												
Blackcap												
Blue Tit												
Brambling												
Brent Goose												
Bullfinch												
Buzzard												
Canada Goose												
Carrion Crow												
Chaffinch												
Chiffchaff												
Coal Tit												
Collared Dove												
Common Gull												
Common Sandpiper												
Common Scoter												
Common Tern												
Coot												
Cormorant												
Crossbill												
Cuckoo												
Curlew												
Curlew Sandpiper												
Dipper												
Dotterel												
Dunlin												

Seasonal Occurrence Chart

	Jan	Feb	Mar	Apr	May	Jun	Jul	Aug	Sept	Oct	Nov	Dec
Dunnock												
Eider												
Fieldfare												
Fulmar												
Gannet												
Garden Warbler												
Garganey												
Glaucous Gull												
Goldcrest												
Golden Plover												
Goldeneye												
Goldfinch												
Goosander												
Goshawk												
Grasshopper Warbler												
Great Black-backed Gull												
Great Crested Grebe												
Great Northern Diver												
Great Skua												
Great Spotted Woodpecker												
Great Tit												
Green Sandpiper												
Green Woodpecker												
Greenfinch												
Greenshank												
Grey Heron												
Grey Partridge												
Grey Plover												
Grey Wagtail												
Greylag Goose												
Guillemot												
Hawfinch												
Hen Harrier												
Herring Gull												
Hobby												
House Martin												
House Sparrow												
Iceland Gull												
Jack Snipe												

	Jan	Feb	Mar	Apr	May	Jun	Jul	Aug	Sept	Oct	Nov	Dec
Jackdaw												
Jay												
Kestrel												
Kingfisher												
Kittiwake												
Knot												
Lapwing												
Leach's Petrel												
Lesser Black-backed Gull												
Lesser Spotted Woodpecker												
Lesser Whitethroat												
Linnet												
Little Grebe												
Little Gull												
Little Owl												
Little Ringed Plover												
Little Stint												
Little Tern												
Long-eared Owl												
Long-tailed Tit												
Mallard												
Manx Shearwater												
Marsh Harrier												
Marsh Tit												
Meadow Pipit												
Mediterranean Gull												
Merlin												
Mistle Thrush												
Moorhen												
Mute Swan												
Nuthatch												
Osprey												
Oystercatcher												
Peregrine												
Pheasant												
Pied Flycatcher												
Pied Wagtail												
Pink-footed Goose												
Pintail												

Seasonal Occurrence Chart

	Jan	Feb	Mar	Apr	May	Jun	Jul	Aug	Sept	Oct	Nov	Dec
Pochard												
Pomarine Skua												
Puffin												
Purple Sandpiper												
Quail												
Raven												
Razorbill												
Red Grouse												
Red-breasted Merganser												
Red-legged Partridge												
Red-throated Diver												
Redpoll												
Redshank												
Redstart												
Redwing												
Reed Bunting												
Reed Warbler												
Ring Ouzel												
Ringed Plover												
Robin												
Rock Dove/Feral Pigeon												
Rock Pipit												
Rook												
Ruddy Duck												
Ruff												
Sand Martin												
Sanderling												
Sandwich Tern												
Scaup												
Sedge Warbler												
Shelduck												
Short-eared Owl												
Shoveler												
Siskin												
Skylark												
Slavonian Grebe												
Smew												
Snipe												
Snow Bunting												

	Jan	Feb	Mar	Apr	May	Jun	Jul	Aug	Sept	Oct	Nov	Dec
Song Thrush												
Sparrowhawk												
Spotted Flycatcher												
Spotted Redshank												
Stock Dove												
Stonechat												
Storm Petrel												
Swallow												
Swift												
Tawny Owl												
Teal												
Tree Pipit												
Tree Sparrow												
Treecreeper												
Tufted Duck												
Turnstone												
Twite												
Water Rail												
Waxwing												
Wheatear												
Whimbrel												
Whinchat												
White Wagtail												
Whitethroat												
Whooper Swan												
Wigeon												
Willow Tit												
Willow Warbler												
Wood Sandpiper												
Wood Warbler												
Woodcock												
Woodpigeon												
Wren												
Yellow Wagtail												
Yellowhammer												

Index

The references in the index refer to walk numbers.

Index